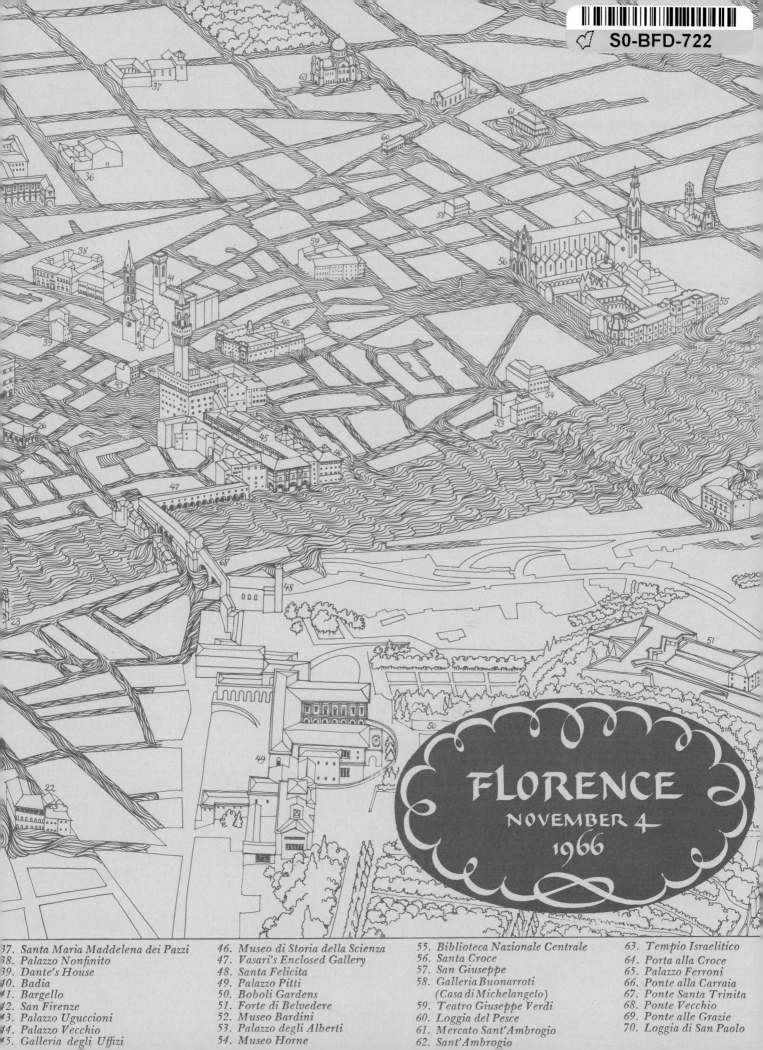

FLORENCE
NOVEMBER 4
1966

37. Santa Maria Maddelena dei Pazzi
38. Palazzo Nonfinito
39. Dante's House
40. Badia
41. Bargello
42. San Firenze
43. Palazzo Uguccioni
44. Palazzo Vecchio
45. Galleria degli Uffizi
46. Museo di Storia della Scienza
47. Vasari's Enclosed Gallery
48. Santa Felicita
49. Palazzo Pitti
50. Boboli Gardens
51. Forte di Belvedere
52. Museo Bardini
53. Palazzo degli Alberti
54. Museo Horne
55. Biblioteca Nazionale Centrale
56. Santa Croce
57. San Giuseppe
58. Galleria Buonarroti
    (Casa di Michelangelo)
59. Teatro Giuseppe Verdi
60. Loggia del Pesce
61. Mercato Sant'Ambrogio
62. Sant'Ambrogio
63. Tempio Israelitico
64. Porta alla Croce
65. Palazzo Ferroni
66. Ponte alla Carraia
67. Ponte Santa Trinita
68. Ponte Vecchio
69. Ponte alle Grazie
70. Loggia di San Paolo

The Waters of November

The Wa

ers of November

Howard Greenfeld

Illustrated with photographs

FOLLETT PUBLISHING COMPANY
Chicago
New York

To Vittoria, a Florentine, with love

Design: John F. Carafoli

© *1969 by Howard Greenfeld*

First Printing H

SBN 695-89183-9 Trade Binding

Library of Congress Catalog Card Number: 69-15098

Contents

	Introduction	7
	Prologue	9
1	November 3, 1966	13
2	The Raging Arno	19
3	Rivers of Mud	31
4	Race Against the Flood	45
5	Appeal for Volunteers	59
6	City in Chaos	71
7	A Dying Masterpiece	85
8	The World Responds	93
9	A Miracle of Recovery	105
10	Miracles of Restoration	109
11	A Hospital for Books	121
12	A Hospital for Paintings	131
13	The Chapel of San Luca	143
	Epilogue	151

Introduction

We live in a time of many disasters: stories of wars, earthquakes, hurricanes, fires and floods fill our daily newspapers. And each disaster is quickly forgotten, replaced by a new and seemingly more dramatic one.

This book is an attempt to record one such disaster, and the world's response to it. The flood waters that raged through Florence in November, 1966, threatened the very existence of a large part of our cultural heritage. Those of us—and there are many—who have profited from our acquaintance with and the knowledge gained from visits to Florence must do all we can to help the great city in its long battle for recovery. We must also do all we can to record exactly what happened during those terrible days, in the hope that it might never happen again.

If one of the reasons that impelled me to write this book is the feeling of a personal debt owed to Florence, for the many ways in which it has enriched my life, I have now incurred a further debt to all the many people in Florence and elsewhere, who have given so unselfishly of their time in the preparation of this book. The Florentines were, without exception, extraordinarily helpful and co-operative in answering my many questions and in showing me what the flood had done to their beloved city. They generously shared their experiences with me, I feel, because they too do not want those disastrous—and heroic—days to be forgotten. Among the many, and I apologize to those I have inadvertently omitted, I especially want to thank Dr. Sergio Camerani,

7

Dr. Giuseppe Pansini and Dr. Francesca Morandini of the State Archives; Professor Alessandro Bonsanti and Dr. Mauro Fabbri of the Gabinetto Vieusseux; Dr. Cristina Piacenti Aschengreen, Dr. Leif Einar Plather and his wife, Dr. Unn Simonson, and Angela Camargo, all of whom helped me understand the complex work of restoration being carried on at the Palazzo Davanzati. Nello Pratolini's account of his personal experiences during the flood was of enormous help, as were the notes kept by Mrs. Cecily Spellman on the work of the volunteers at the Certosa. The students of Florence, among the unexpected heroes of the flood (though their courage and dedication does not surprise me), were both articulate and perceptive in speaking of the days following the disaster, and my special thanks go to eight of them: Enrico Guaita, Tommaso Detti, Riccardo Francovich, Mario Pachi, Valerio Valoriani, Sergio Marchini, Roberto Salvadori and Giancarlo Galardini. I am grateful, too, for the co-operation of Bruno Tassi, Barbara Bannon, Betty Troubh, Alice Cromie, Eleanor Levieux, Freda Barry Brown, Helena Strassova, and Dora Vallier.

The Committee to Rescue Italian Art, which has done such an outstanding job, helped me at every stage, and I must give special thanks to Professor Felton L. Gibbons and Judith Munat of the CRIA office in Florence. I am grateful, as well, to Michel Conil Lacoste of UNESCO for his encouragement and information.

I would never have undertaken to write this book without the initial enthusiasm of my editor, Mrs. Esther K. Meeks. And I owe very special thanks to four people who went out of their way to make gathering this material an extremely pleasant task while I was in Florence; I very much enjoyed working with them: Anne Boardman, Maria Luigia Guaita, Judith Green, and Ron Cunningham.

Florence, 1968   H. G.

Prologue

On November 1, 1966, Maria Luigia Guaita, founder and guiding spirit of "Il Bisonte," the finest lithography workshop in Italy, well-known throughout the world, was given a nineteenth-century drawing to restore. The drawing was in poor condition, but she felt sure that she and her highly competent workmen could do the job; besides, it was of special interest to her. It showed her district, San Niccolò, on the morning of an important and tragic day in the history of Florence, the day of the flood of 1844. Reporting that flood, the contemporary historian Giuseppe Aiazzi had written: "It is foolhardy, perhaps, to attempt a description of how the River Arno without warning overflowed its banks, flooded the streets, squares and houses of much of our city, and brought sudden terror to much of our population. Mere words can paint no true picture of the many tragic scenes which we have witnessed. . . . On the left bank of the Arno, the flood entered by the Porta San Niccolò. . . ."

The section of Florence known as San Niccolò is one of the poorest and noblest of the city, almost totally ignored by tourists. It is the quarter of small artisans, workers in leather, gold, and silver, who have done so much to make the handicraft of Florence known throughout the world. Rich as it is in history, as the city of Dante, Leonardo da Vinci, Michelangelo, Galileo, Machiavelli, and Giotto, the proud tradition of Florence is carried into modern times by its skilled artisans and their exquisite, hand-wrought products. It was for this reason that Maria Luigia Guaita had chosen San Niccolò as the site for her studio, for

Borgo S. Niccolò
La mattina del 3 Novembre 1844

she too had an absolute respect for the ancient traditions and rules of her art, that of lithography. By holding scrupulously to the classical procedures, with the use of hand presses and especially made paper, she was faithfully producing the works of the finest modern artists, using centuries-old methods of artisan production.

Signorina Guaita carefully examined the drawing to be restored. It showed her street, via San Niccolò, as an angry torrent. The flood waters are carrying chairs, tables, boxes in their wake. In the middle of the street is a boat; in the boat are men handing out food supplies to the people leaning from the windows, terrified looks on their faces, most of them holding baskets at the end of ropes, baskets in which to collect the food.

At the bottom of the print, the title: BORGO SAN NICCOLÒ, LA MATTINA DEL 3 NOVEMBRE 1844 (THE MORNING OF NOVEMBER 3, 1844).

1

November 3, 1966

On November 3, 1966, a heavy rain poured down upon Florence. It had been a terrible period, gray, cloudy and, above all, wet since October 25th. The week-long showers had seemingly come to an end the morning of November 1st. But now they were starting again, heavier than ever.

Nonetheless, the Florentines were happy. It was Thursday, and that evening they would begin a three-day weekend, for the following day, the fourth, was Armed Forces Day, a national holiday celebrating the Italian victory in World War I, forty-eight years before. And then, Saturday and Sunday, to make a long weekend.

The rain-drenched tricolor Italian flag was flying from the buildings along with the fleur-de-lys, the symbol of the great city of Florence. People were making their final plans for the days ahead, doing their last-minute shopping for the holidays. Already the stores on the elegant via Tornabuoni were displaying their Christmas wares. In the cafés, the people sipped their hot, dark coffee, talked of the holiday weekend, exchanged views on a spectacular bank robbery that had taken place in a neighboring town the day before, and gossiped— Florentines for centuries have been well-known for the latter. Occasionally, they discussed the terrible weather, but usually in terms of their vacations that would or would not be postponed because of the rain.

Little attention was paid to reports of swelling waters in the tributaries that fed the Arno, the river that flows through Florence.

There had been stories of flooding in the countryside, but this could hardly be a threat to Florence itself. History had reported several major floods in the city's past, but the last one was in 1844, and surely new and modern methods had been devised to prevent a recurrence of such a disaster.

The bad weather evidently had done little to reduce the exodus from the city, and by seven o'clock the streets leading out of town, towards the highways, were jammed. Around the Piazza del Duomo, site of the magnificent 500-year-old, multi-colored cathedral, the cars were at a standstill. Motorists were stalled near the famed Baptistry, where Dante had been baptized, and whose door, by Lorenzo Ghiberti, is known as the Gate of Paradise. Traffic, too, normally bad and made even worse by the pounding rainfall, was snarled in the streets leading to Piazza Santa Croce.

While those Florentines fortunate enough to be able to leave the city for the long weekend were making their way to the country, the tourists who had come to Florence from all over the world were carefully studying their guidebooks to make plans for the following days. Florence has long been a center for both the casual visitor and the serious student. Few cities in the world offer such riches. The museums alone, such as the Uffizi, the Pitti, the National Museum (or Bargello), contain the finest treasures of that period between the fourteenth and sixteenth centuries known as the Renaissance, marked by a new spirit of curiosity and interest in man and all his surroundings—works by such masters as Michelangelo, Leonardo da Vinci, Botticelli, and Raphael. And the numerous churches, themselves masterpieces of architecture, house some of the greatest works of art ever produced by man: sculptures and frescoes (wall paintings) and paintings by Giotto, Botticelli, Cimabue, Fra Angelico, Andrea Del Sarto, Donatello, and Masaccio, to mention only a very few. The streets of Florence themselves, lined with powerful gray, brown and yellow stone buildings have caused the entire city to be called a living museum. For the serious student and researcher, there are the facilities of the immensely rich National Library (Biblioteca Nazionale), the famed State Archives, the

A view of Florence from Piazzale Michelangelo, before the flood. To the right is the Duomo, in the center the Campanile, and at the left the Palazzo Vecchio

shelves of the Gabinetto Vieusseux—a fundamental source for nineteenth-century documents. To remind the visitor of the Renaissance discovery of the new sciences, there is a uniquely important Museum of the History of Science. And for others, there are the splendid shops displaying those leather and silver goods which have brought world-wide fame and respect to the modern Florentine craftsman.

The native Florentine is always, inevitably, aware of the heritage of his great city, is reminded of it at every street corner. His tastes, his very way of life are affected—even if unconsciously—by the beauties amidst which he lives. He is known to be proud, rather haughty, and he feels himself somewhat superior to other Italians and, indeed, to the rest of the world. He may be a citizen of the world, a citizen of Italy, but he is, above all, a Florentine.

Yet for him the pleasures of the first night of a long holiday weekend were not unlike those enjoyed by people all over the world. There was, of course, one reminder of the wonders of the Florentine past; a concert to be given in the magnificent Salone dei Cinquecento (Hall of the Five Hundred), built by Giorgio Vasari, the painter, architect and biographer of the great Renaissance artists, in the Palazzo Vecchio, the city hall whose tower rises high above the city. The concert was to be given that Thursday night; the following day, there would be a holiday flag-raising ceremony in the famous square, Piazza della Signoria, on which the Palazzo Vecchio stands.

However, most Florentines who were spending the long weekend in Florence were either at home watching television, playing cards or merely spending the evening in the company of friends. Those who did venture out in the pouring rain went to the movies—a favorite occupation for Florentines, since other entertainments such as night clubs are few in their city. Of all the movie houses in town, none drew a larger crowd than did the Teatro Verdi, a theater more than one hundred years old, which was showing *The Bible*. In spite of the heavy downpour, long lines of moviegoers formed, ready to be thrilled by the spectacular scenes of the Deluge and the building of Noah's Ark.

On the outskirts of town, the soldiers spent the evening in their barracks, polishing their boots. Already the tanks and vehicles were gleaming. The soldiers were tired, having spent hours in the rain working to prepare for the great parade.

Maria Luigia Guaita spent the afternoon of November 3rd rearranging her new home above and adjoining her lithography workshop. The apartment consisted of a spacious living and reception room and a dining room, both of which faced a small garden in the courtyard just a few yards from the river, a newly equipped kitchen; and, one flight above, reached by an inner stairway, a light and sunny bedroom, its walls brightened by a brilliant collection of modern Italian paintings, and a bathroom with a small barred window looking out on the central staircase of the building. Across that main staircase was a room and bath which also belonged to Signorina Guaita, occupied by her young nephew Enrico. Everything in the apartment sparkled; it was all new—the heating, the linens, the lights, and the furniture. It was, for this extraordinarily dynamic woman, the fruit of a lifetime of hard work, work which had been rewarded by her international success as a person who has carried forward into modern times the artistic skills of the ancient Florentines.

That afternoon, a workman, who had been putting finishing touches on the apartment, came into the living room and told Signorina Guaita that there was water in the basement. Going downstairs with him, she saw a thin line of water trickling from the walls. Nothing to worry about, he assured her. The basements of the houses of San Niccolò were often flooded; after all, the Arno runs close by through an embankment of earth, and the sewage system in that part of town is as old as Florence itself. Yet, nothing serious had ever happened; the water reaches a peak and goes away.

The workman went home and, a few hours later, Signorina Guaita went back down to the basement. The level had risen considerably, and a rather strong jet of water was now coming through the walls. Worried this time, she called the local mason who had helped her construct her apartment. It must be a leaking shower pipe, the mason said, but the water was only four inches high, not very unusual, and there was a drainage shaft in the basement in case it went too high. The only precaution to be taken concerned the newly installed oil burner, around which the mason put a protective wall of sacks.

In the evening, a few friends braved the downpour to come in to celebrate the completion of the new apartment. They toasted, with a bottle of champagne, the success of Maria Luigia Guaita in her new home. By midnight they had left, and Signorina Guaita went to sleep in her new bed. The sound of the heavy rains unnerved her a bit, and to help her sleep she took a light sleeping pill.

2

The Raging Arno

It continued to rain throughout the night of November 3rd; the people of Florence went to bed concerned, but totally unsuspecting what would happen to them and their city. The Arno and its tributaries, particularly the Sieve just upstream from the city, grew even more swollen. By the first dim light of dawn the level of the river had risen far above the danger point and the arches of the lovely bridges that span the Arno had been completely blocked. As the raging Arno rushed towards the sea, it dragged in its wake tree trunks, beams, furniture, tires, household goods of all sorts, even the swollen corpses of animals, battering the embankments and bridges in its fury. It seemed, according to one eye witness, a gigantic steamroller that destroyed, crushed, and annihilated everything in its path.

Very few Florentines witnessed this horrifying sight—only a few night watchmen, bakers, and perhaps those few citizens who had celebrated the holiday eve with a visit to a night club. Except for the jewelers on the fabled Ponte Vecchio—the 600-year-old bridge on which the shops of Florence's finest gold and silver craftsmen are found—who were alerted by their own private night watchman about the potential danger to their small shops, the people of Florence slept unaware of what was happening just outside their homes.

At three in the morning, Nello Pratolini awoke in his apartment on the via San Niccolò, not far from the workshop and home of Maria Luigia Guaita. From his window he could see the lightning

and hear the thunder that was rumbling in the distance. The rain, incredibly, was even heavier than it had been when he went to sleep. He went back to bed but was unable to sleep. The flashes of lightning increased and filtered through the windows of the living room, and the rain drummed on the loosened tiles of the extended roof of the apartment below his. Finally he fell asleep, worried.

A few hours later, Pratolini, his wife, and his son awoke with a start. The noise outside was terrifying, and they all rushed to the kitchen window from which they could see out into via San Niccolò. What they saw was a slimy "canal" of water which had covered the entire length of their street. The sidewalks had disappeared completely, and the water had risen above the wheels of all the parked cars—including Pratolini's own.

The first thought that occurred to the Pratolini family was that the water main had broken again, as it had all too often in the past, pouring pure drinking water into the streets. But this time the water was too dirty, and the current far too fast. While Pratolini and his son quickly dressed, Signora Pratolini remained at the window. Friends and neighbors had by that time gathered at their windows too. "What's going on?" cried one voice. "It's the pipes," answered a voice from the "canal" below, where the figure of a man in high rubber boots could be seen moving with difficulty through the water, trying desperately to get to his car.

It was about six A.M. when Pratolini and his son raced downstairs. The entrance to their building was already full of water, and when they reached the street they found themselves up to their knees in the dark, slimy torrent. The car was in front of the house, parked along what had been a sidewalk the night before. Though almost paralyzed with fear, they managed to push the car to what they thought was a safe place not far away. They were not alone; it seemed that every car owner on the street was doing the same thing.

The water was continuing to rise, and a rumor spread through the block that the Arno was threatening to break over the parapets. Young Pratolini decided to venture out further, to take a look for

23

There was a lake in front of the Baptistry

himself, while his father, with great effort, made his way back to the house to rejoin his wife at the window.

The interminable night seemed to be ending as the daylight grew. From their window the Pratolinis looked down the street. They saw their son, waist high in water, frantically signaling and shouting amidst what was now a din. Soon he returned, covered with mud and slime; he confirmed what they had already known. The Arno was overflowing; across the river from via San Niccolò the ugly yellow water was rushing through the streets. They were all at the mercy of the river, so often eulogized in song, that Elisabeth Barrett Browning wrote of as flowing "like a crystal arrow."

When he had cleaned off the mud, Pratolini's son joined his parents at the window. It was now daytime, and the rain was still coming down. The water continued to rise and began to invade the first shops. The parked cars were by now completely submerged, and the tall doorways of the old buildings were more than half under water. The people of San Niccolò were marooned, helpless. The tenants on the lower floors hurried to their neighbors upstairs; their own apartments were threatened by the rising waters, and those possessions left behind would be destroyed.

Pratolini went up to the fifth-floor apartment of his friend, the oldest tenant in the building, Mario Tizianini. From Tizianini's window he was able to see the destruction being wrought by the flood. The waters were reaching his own car, his most valued possession.

"We came back downstairs to the women," Pratolini has written. "I shall never forget old Tosca's fright; the dignified tears of the old florist from the second floor, his son's dismay and his mother's restiveness; the convulsive trembling of my wife; and the uncontrollable terror of Tizianini's wife who kept repeating: 'But in Santa Croce—the hotel—oh, my God—my grandchildren.' My son's face had become darker as his thoughts ran to his fiancée Grazia and her family, who were at San Màuro a Sìgna, a small village downstream from Florence, where things were surely even worse.

"By now we were barricaded by more than ten feet of water;

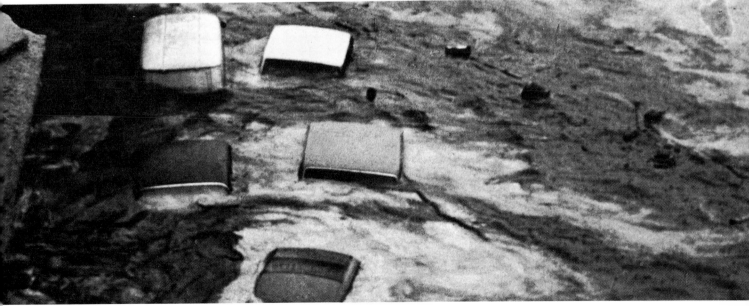

the street had become a river. Antonietta began to bring her things from a lower floor into our apartment: mattresses, chairs, the television set, many small but nonetheless cherished things; the water was still climbing the stairway. I had another look at my car; we could no longer hope, for it was being totally submerged.

"The little piazza at the end of the street had become an artificial lake. Like volcanoes, two huge arches beyond the gate at the end of the street spewed forth more of the yellowish water that was flooding the whole area, while the rain continued to pour down. My car was finally swallowed up."

Pratolini's car was the last in the neighborhood to go under. The raging waters had by then filled all the stores, the favorite neighborhood café had disappeared, and the water lapped at the awning above the local grocery store. The dry cleaner's shop, too, vanished and with it all the clothes the Pratolini family had just brought in to be cleaned.

At 7:26 in the morning all electric clocks stopped in Florence. The city was cut off from the rest of the world. On his small transister radio, Pratolini was able to hear the news: "Florence is a lake."

There was nothing to do but wait in terror for what might happen next. Soon the great floodtide came as the Arno broke through its banks. "From our observation post in Mario Tizianini's fifth-floor apartment," Pratolini went on, "we watched the terrifying spectacle of the great mass of water which hurled itself like a muddy tidal wave into the bowels of our street, swelling the slimy waters even more. I will never forget the sight of that terrible moment, with its chorus of screams of horror from the people nailed to their window sills. Cars were lifted up and tossed from wall to wall. Window frames and huge heavy doors torn from heaven knows what ancient palace floated by like sheets of paper, along with an enormous number of car and truck tires, immense piles of all sorts of wood, precious volumes from the bookstores, mattresses and all kinds of household goods—all began to float by our windows for hours, carried off with devastating fury by the terrible waters of the Arno."

Streets became canals

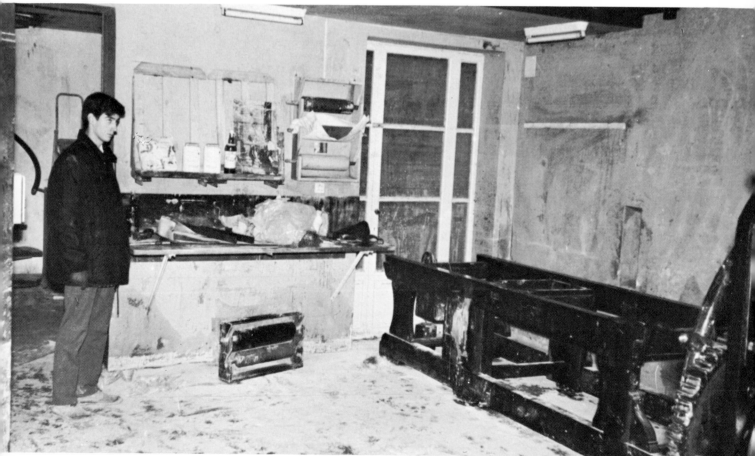

The waters had reached those apartments on the second floor. By early afternoon, the via San Niccolò had disappeared under sixteen feet of water. The sky darkened and the swollen rainclouds above continued to pour their water upon the city. Down below, the river continued its work of destruction, with fuel oil released from the basement tanks giving it the air of an oily red-and-black serpent.

Via San Niccolò was now a navigable river, and wild applause greeted the appearance of the first little rubber boat which fought against the current, with Titti, owner of the cleaning store, and a young friend aboard. It was these two young men who brought the first words of comfort to San Niccolò. Seemingly indifferent to the risk they were running, they sailed down the length of the street, shouting up words of encouragement to the people leaning out of their windows, promising to bring milk, water, bread to the needy, agreeing to relay messages to friends and relatives outside the district, as they steered their boat through the roofs of submerged cars.

As night fell on San Niccolò, the residents still trembled with fear. How could they survive the night half-submerged in water? From time to time, the light from a small flashlight appeared below, the light from the small rubber raft, going its rounds to help the people of San Niccolò.

Down the street from the home of Nello Pratolini, Maria Luigia Guaita had awakened at eight in the morning as usual. At her window she heard a sound of dripping.

She pulled up the blinds and saw that her garden was flooded with muddy water. Unable to see the street from her window, and thus unaware what had happened, she was sure that the water was coming from under the earth. She hurried down the stairs, into her living room. The two large windows that faced into the garden from her living room seemed to be threatened by the waters from outside. Still certain that this was a local disorder, she nonetheless picked up an ancient soup tureen, a watercolor by the modern Italian painter Giorgio Morandi, and a photo of her mother and carried them upstairs.

29

The reception room of Il Bisonte, a few days after the flood
(Bottom) The workshop of Il Bisonte, after the flood

She again looked out the window; from it she saw the water breaking through her living room windows. She was desperate. From the bathroom, she heard a noise. Running to it, she found her nephew Enrico on the other side, breaking down the grille work of the small bathroom window. He begged her to come through it and escape the waters that would soon flood her home and workshop. The water had by then reached her bedroom. Literally swimming about, she grabbed what she could—more valuable paintings, some cups that were floating in the slime; even, irrationally, a pillow which she passed through the bathroom window to Enrico. Finally, she swam out through the window into Enrico's arms. Together they climbed to the top floor, to the apartment of a retired railway worker. From the railway worker's window she finally saw what had happened to her beloved San Niccolò. It was a raging torrent; cars, wardrobes, oil cans, cupboards, doors, and windows were rushing with the flow. An elderly woman caught in the whirlpool was rescued when a rope was lowered from a window by means of which she was pulled out of the water.

Maria Luigia Guaita, strangely, felt no despair. Instead, a feeling of euphoria came over her. She had been saved; the perilous adventure was over. Only later on Saturday evening when she and Enrico returned downstairs, did she realize that a great deal of Il Bisonte— much of her equipment, most of her paintings and lithographs—had been destroyed, or at least seriously damaged. As she and Enrico made their way through the water, slime, and mud which covered the workshop and living room, they were almost overcome by the smell of oil. At their feet, among floating paintings and lithographs, fish were swimming. Heavy hand presses had been displaced by the impact, and zinc and copper plates were buried in sludge. Lithographs were pressed to the mud-smeared walls like handkerchiefs. As Maria Luigia Guaita waded through the mud, desperately seeking to salvage what she could, she knew the struggle to rebuild Il Bisonte would be a difficult one—but she never doubted the outcome.

3

Rivers of Mud

On November 4, 1966, the center of Florence was turned into a muddy, desolate swamp. Florence, the city in which Dante and Petrarch had written their verses and in which Boccaccio had penned his tales.... It was in Florence that Galileo had changed man's concept of the universe and that Machiavelli had altered man's political thought. It was in Florence that some of the greatest painters, sculptors, and architects had flourished, leaving to their beloved city a magnificent part of their legacy so that the present-day visitor to Florence can still imagine himself to be in the city of Michelangelo and Leonardo da Vinci.

On November 4, Florence was buried under 500,000 tons of mud—approximately one ton per inhabitant. The mud filled houses and cellars, and it blocked the city's drainage system. As if the onslaught of mud were not enough, the thick layer of dark, heavy fuel oil had turned the flood waters into a thick, greasy soup. The torrent ripped at parked cars, hurling them against shops and smashing them into stone walls. Trees, doors, traffic lights, gates and furniture were swept along by the raging current. More than six thousand stores were destroyed, their iron shutters bashed in, their windows broken, their merchandise covered with black oil and mud. In the streets lay sodden leather goods and furs, ripped and oil-stained clothing, swollen tables and chairs, broken plates and bottles.

Houses collapsed throughout the city. The newspaper plant was destroyed. Patients were stranded in the dark, cold clinics and hospi-

The cloister at the Church of
Santa Croce, before the flood

The same cloister,
after the flood

tals, where food and medicine were in short supply. The jails were flooded and prisoners released—some of them joined in the effort to rescue their fellow citizens, and some of them escaped. At the race-track, 120 thoroughbred horses were drowned, and at the zoo countless animals were drowned in the water or buried in the mud.

At about nine in the evening, the waters receded, but a long and terrible night was to follow. Florence was still cut off from the world. Roads leading to the city were blocked, and telephone communication was impossible. There was no electricity, and the cold rain which continued to pour down chilled the heatless homes. In the sky, helicopters hovered to rescue the desperate survivors who were stranded on rooftops. Down below, firemen and volunteers paddled rubber boats and rafts through the streets to rescue and bring aid to victims of the flood. Four thousand families were homeless, and eleven thousand had suffered serious losses.

The city was putrid with the smell of fuel oil, rotting garbage, and the carcasses of dead animals. And throughout the night, the wailing of car horns was heard, for the waters had short-circuited the automobiles' electrical systems.

It had been a day of tragedy, but on the following morning, the citizens of Florence were concerned not only with their own welfare and possessions, but also the fate of the treasures which were housed in the city's churches, museums and libraries.

Early on Friday morning, the furious waters had reached the popular district of Santa Croce. It is a poor section of narrow thirteenth-century streets and dark, cold houses, but it is filled with a vitality and charm special to its colorful inhabitants. Dominating the district is one of the largest and best-known churches of Florence, the Church of Santa Croce, begun in 1295. Because it contains the tombs of Michelangelo, Machiavelli, Galileo, and Rossini as well as countless other renowned Italians, Santa Croce is often called Italy's Westminster Abbey. It also holds some of the most valued treasure of Florentine art.

*Interior of Santa Croce,
the most famous
Franciscan church in Italy,
an architectural monument
which suffered severely
from the flood*

*(Next page)
Priests stuff old bedding
and sacking into the cracks
of the door of their church
as the waters rise*

A little after six in the morning, Father Gustavo Cocci, the Franciscan Prior of Santa Croce, opened a small door to leave the basilica; he was to go to a chapel to say early mass. As the door opened, a rush of water entered the church. Before slamming the door shut, he saw that the enormous square in front of the church was already filled with the swirling water. It was rising around the statue of Dante in the center, and it carried with it mud, oil, debris; it was already covering the cars parked in the square. With the aid of monks, Father Cocci hurriedly bolted the huge doors to the church. They held for a few short hours, but finally the waters invaded the magnificent building, carrying the ever-present mud and oil with them, rising to a level of nearly nine feet, and staining the marble statues and tombs that line the walls of the church. The waters then entered the superb Pazzi Chapel, an example of architectural perfection by Filippo Brunelleschi, causing serious damage to that great architect and sculptor's masterpiece. And from below, the intense water pressure in the cellar caused a room of the famed museum of Santa Croce to explode, submerging Cimabue's *Crucifix* and seriously damaging Taddeo Gaddi's powerful fresco of *The Last Supper*.

Early in the morning, too, the waters rushed towards the Church of Ognissanti, a thirteenth-century building considerably altered in the seventeenth century, which holds the tomb of Sandro Botticelli, as well as several outstanding examples of religious art. Inside the church were seventeen Franciscan priests and monks. As they heard the sound of the approaching waters, they quickly bolted the heavy wooden door. To make it more secure, they worked feverishly to build an added barrier to the waters by piling benches high against the doors. It was hopeless. An immense wave overcame the results of their anguished labors, beating down the iron-bolted door, hurling the benches in every direction with enormous force as it exploded into the church. The flood smashed everything in sight, uprooting the church organ. The waters rose to a level of eight feet, leaving thick oil deposits on works by Botticelli and Ghirlandaio.

Many other churches, too, felt the fury of the flood. Over eleven

*Scene of destruction in front
of Santa Maria Novella*

*(Next page)
The interior
of Santa Maria Novella
after the flood*

Disaster in the
Piazza del Duomo

feet of water desecrated one of Florence's oldest churches, Sant' Ambrogio, half immersing the nave altarpiece and seriously damaging several important works of art by Florentine masters. In the eleventh-century church of Santissimi Apostili, the water rose to more than fourteen feet, leaving behind a pile of mud and debris three feet high when it retreated. Every object in the nave was damaged or destroyed; the tabernacle attributed to Della Robbia was covered with mud and oil. Seriously damaged, too, were the altarpieces, and a major work by Giorgio Vasari, *The Immaculate Conception*, whose panel was split and distorted and which suffered serious paint losses.

Huge amounts of sludge mixed with debris and oil left their marks on the lovely church and cloisters of Santa Maria Maddalena de' Pazzi, harming a precious fresco by Perugino and his pupils. Hard hit by the water as well was one of the most important churches of Florence, the beautiful Santa Maria Novella. It stands on a large square near the railroad station and was built in the form of an Egyptian cross, with a nave and two aisles. This church was severely attacked, the angry waters flooding the nave and leaving thick coats of oil on the famed frescoes in its Spanish Chapel, Strozzi Chapel and Green Cloister.

By late morning, three ferocious torrents of oil-infested, debris-filled water converged upon the Piazza del Duomo at a speed of more than forty miles an hour. The waters mercilessly pounded at the Baptistry, beating relentlessly against its famous doors. On the south side, two of the twenty-eight panels from a heavy bronze door, made by Andrea Pisano in 1336, were torn away. And on the east side, the most famous door in Florence, the magnificent Gate of Paradise, so named by Michelangelo, was shaken by the vibrations of the waters which battered it. This immense, heavy door consists of ten gilded bronze panels, the work of a Florentine sculptor and goldsmith, Lorenzo Ghiberti, who spent twenty-seven years in the first half of the fifteenth century making them. These brilliant and dramatic panels depict ten stories from the Old Testament: The Creation of Adam and Eve, Cain killing Abel, Jacob and Esau, Joseph being sold into slavery by his brothers, King Solomon and the Queen of Sheba, Noah's Drunkenness, the Sacrifice of Isaac, Moses on Mount Sinai, the Siege of Jericho, and David and Goliath. Of these, the first five were brutally dislodged. Fortunately they were swept against a wrought-iron fence which surrounds the medieval building and because of this recovered from the mud. Their exquisite reliefs had been scratched and stained with oil, but they were intact and could be restored with careful cleaning.

The deadly waters continued sweeping into the Baptistry itself, rising to more than seven feet and damaging Donatello's superb fifteenth-century carved wood sculpture of Mary Magdalene. Across the street, the flood tore into the Duomo, the cathedral, rising to five feet in the nave, wrecking the pavements of both sacristies, making a shattered raft of two hundred movable pews, seriously damaging two organs and inundating a painting of *The Last Supper* by Giovanni Balducci, which had been temporarily placed in the cellar for restoration.

4

Race Against the Flood

The museums of Florence, too, took the full impact of the flood. Terror reigned at the Uffizi, the world's most important gallery of Renaissance art, and its collection was saved only by the courage and determination of a small group of men and women. The gigantic building was constructed by Giorgio Vasari between 1560 and 1574 as a government office (*Uffizi* means offices in Italian). Later it was converted into a museum to house the large collection of Renaissance art. Ironically, Vasari built it near the Arno so that from every part of it one could be reminded of the presence of the river, the pride of Florence.

At about seven in the morning of November 4th, the gallery's watchman notified Dr. Luisa Becherucci, the director of the museum, of the pending danger. She in turn called Professor Ugo Procacci, an eminent art historian and Superintendent of Fine Arts for the Florentine region, who contacted Dr. Umberto Baldini, Director of Restorations, and other members of the staff. They all hurried to the museum to find that the river which had been the pride of the city had become its ruin. Fortunately, the greatest masterpieces in the museum were on the top floors; it was unlikely that the waters could ever reach that high. However, the two large restoration laboratories, connected to the Uffizi and located in the basements, were threatened. To these laboratories come some of the finest paintings and frescoes of Florence and of all Italy, sent to Florence to be restored and mended. The art of restoration has flourished there for many years, and the Florentine restorers are among the finest in the world.

Dr. Becherucci, Professor Procacci, and the others rushed to one of the workshops and found upon their arrival that it was too late—the water had already reached the ceiling, and there was nothing to be done. Only the heavy doors, standing against the surging waters, prevented the paintings from being carried out to the streets.

Undaunted, the small group made their way to a second laboratory, located in the old post office. There paintings and statues were already afloat, but rescue work could be attempted. Time was running out, however, as the water rose, and an immediate selection had to be made: which paintings were to be removed first and which, through this selection, might be condemned to death? These were difficult decisions, and there was no time for lengthy consideration. The group turned to Professor Procacci, who assumed the painful responsibility of choosing among the many paintings, each one representing something very special and personal to the band of rescuers. The necessary decisions were made and, following Procacci's orders, the paintings—heavy, bulky and hard to handle—were relayed, from hand to hand, to high places, on top of cupboards or up the staircase. It was a race against time, as the waters continued to rise and the perils increased.

The group of museum experts and workers had grown in the course of the morning with the arrival of four student volunteers. Some of these were sent by Professor Procacci to find pumps to aid in the essential job of clearing out the basements. However, their missions were unsuccessful; pumps were being used to save the scores of human beings in danger throughout the city, and none were available for works of art.

The dangerous, exhausting work continued, as Procacci and his group moved on to the museum's storeroom, at the Romanesque church of San Piero Scheraggio nearby, where more than two hundred works of exceptional value were awaiting restoration, among them *The Coronation of the Virgin* by Botticelli. There, too, it was a race against the waters which poured in. And to complicate matters, the priceless masterpieces could be reached only after breaking down a heavy iron grating. But Procacci and his helpers broke through the grating and

46

A view of tragedy in the Uffizi restoration rooms

Damaged works of art in the Uffizi

again began their task of moving paintings out and up, to safe, dry places.

Suddenly, Procacci announced that he was going to the Vasari gallery. The men and women working with him looked horrified. The Vasari gallery is a corridor which links the Uffizi with another museum, the Pitti Palace across the river, running above the Ponte Vecchio. Under the old bridge, the river raged; there seemed little hope that it could survive the steady attack of the pounding waters. One high wave, and the bridge would collapse and with it the precious collection of self-portraits, including works by Raphael, Titian, Rubens, and Corot, which were hanging in the corridor above the bridge.

Procacci knew he had to risk his own life to save these paintings; it was a job he alone had to do, one he could not ask of others, for the personal dangers were too great.

But as Procacci set out, his co-workers joined him. Again human chains were formed; masterpiece after masterpiece was passed along, out of the corridor, as the flood waters stormed below. The dangerous job was completed; all of the paintings were removed from the corridor. Fortunately, the Ponte Vecchio, battered and ancient, held. The waters lost force by rushing through the stores that lined the bridge. They destroyed these small shops, but the bridge, and thus the corridor, held firm. But even if it had risen and destroyed the bridge, the paintings would have been saved by the courage of this small group.

Professor Procacci, Dr. Becherucci, Dr. Baldini and the others kept up their exhausting work till early the morning of the following day. When they finally left for their homes, they knew they had done all that was humanly possible to save a major part of the heritage of Florence.

Near the Uffizi stands a unique monument to man's search for knowledge through science, the National Museum of the History of Science. Included in its collection are Edison's phonograph, ancient compasses, Galileo's telescopes, including the one through which he first saw the planets of Jupiter, an important collection of celestial and

(Next page) Floods battered the Ponte Vecchio, but the bridge held

terrestial globes dating from the eighth to the seventeenth centuries, Brambilla's surgical instruments of ivory, gold, and ebony, and a vast collection of old maps, clocks, and astrolabes.

The director of the museum, Dr. Maria Luisa Righini Bonelli, worked late the night of November 3rd. Since her husband was in Brazil at the time, she decided to sleep in the museum's small ground-floor apartment. In the morning she was awakened by a sound of rushing water. The tide had come through her window and was already at the level of her bed. Horrified, she ran about the ground floor of the museum, breathlessly gathering what she could of the invaluable collection and bringing it to the floors above. Forming whirlpools of foam, the water was sweeping away the anatomy rooms and their contents, the electrostatic apparatus, optical instruments and instruments of cosmography and astronomy. Time and again Dr. Bonelli returned to the ground floor, filled her arms with precious original instruments used by the founders of modern chemistry, physics, and medicine, and carried them upstairs. But the waters rose, bringing with them the suffocating smell of fuel oil. The struggle had to be abandoned; many objects were left to the mercies of the flood, but Dr. Bonelli had done a heroic job of salvaging many of the museum's smaller treasures, including several of Galileo's telescopes.

The waters invaded the home of Amerigo Vespucci, for whom America was named, as well as the Casa Buonarroti, which had been bought by Michelangelo for his nephew and decorated in the seventeenth century with episodes from the life of the artist. There two paintings by Bronzino and Battista Franco were almost ruined and a collection of portraits of Michelangelo immersed and covered with mud.

The situation in the Archeological Museum nearby was catastrophic. The furious waters first entered the cellars of the great museum, causing the explosion of the ground floor, the thirty-four rooms of which were then submerged in six feet of oily water. The glass cases in the middle of the rooms, holding precious collections of Etruscan pots, vases and other valuable relics, were demolished, their treasures

The entrance to Casa Buonarroti

dispersed, buried in the mud, or sucked into the cellars. Over nine thousand objects were seriously damaged.

The story in the other important Florentine museums was the same. The waters which flooded the ground floor of the Bardini Museum gravely damaged an important collection of the sixteenth- to nineteenth-century musical instruments as well as a superb *Madonna* by Luca Cranach. The water rose to a height of thirteen feet in the National Museum, the Bargello, lashing out against the walls of the ground floor, and imperiling the library and offices as well as the elegant courtyard.

In the library of the hundred-year-old Cherubini conservatory of music, two shelves of musical manuscripts from the sixteenth to nineteenth centuries, including unpublished manuscripts by Gioacchino Rossini, composer of *The Barber of Seville,* were inundated and damaged.

In another part of the city, over fourteen feet of mud and water entered the Horne Museum, which was donated to Florence by an English scholar and collector, Herbert Percy Horne, in 1916. The museum is known for its outstanding collection of fourteenth- and fifteenth-century paintings as well as a superb collection of household objects of historical importance. It suffered badly; several paintings were damaged, one hundred volumes of fourteenth- to eighteenth-century archives were saturated and splendid Renaissance furniture and woodwork partially destroyed.

Florence's magnificent libraries, too, were brutally attacked. The Gabinetto Vieusseux, a library founded in 1819, specializing in literature of the eighteenth and nineteenth centuries, had grown to become the largest lending library in Italy. Directed by a quiet, scholarly novelist, Professor Alessandro Bonsanti, it became a rich source of French, English, and American literature. Located in the noble Palazzo Strozzi, its collection was largely kept underground; so it was completely submerged the morning of November 4th. The water came with such violence that books were hurled to the ceiling, where they remained as if glued. Word spread throughout the city, and students

*The army helped with the
rescue work*

came, formed human chains, going from the basement to higher floors, relaying the mud-soaked books to the safer areas of the beautifully proportioned fifteenth-century palace.

Most dramatic of all, perhaps, was the scene at the world-famed National Library, which experienced the greatest disaster to befall any library in modern times. The National Library is one of the most important in the world; founded in the first half of the eighteenth century, it houses well over a million books as well as one of the great collections of incunabulae and illuminated manuscripts. Among its treasures are letters by Michelangelo and Machiavelli as well as three hundred volumes of Galileo's papers. On the morning of November 4th, the director of the National Library, Dr. Emanuele Casamassima, was at his home, to the south of Florence. Notified of the flood by a colleague, he rushed into the city. The library stood near the banks of the Arno; it was taking the full force of the flood. But Casamassima found himself on the opposite bank of the river, helpless, unable to cross the bridge to reach his library. He spent the entire day in a desperate attempt to get amphibious means to cross the river, but to no avail; not until early on the morning of the 5th was he able to reach his precious library. And then there, as at the Vieusseux, students arrived, seemingly from out of nowhere, to offer their help to drag the invaluable books and manuscripts and documents from the mud.

Conditions were dreadful at the library. Fumes from the mud and slime were so strong that many of the students had to wear gas masks as they passed the books up from the lower floors of the old library. From there they were transported to tobacco barns, brick kilns and textile plants to be dried out. Next, they were carried in truckloads to the Renaissance Fort Belvedere, on a high hill south of the city. At the fort they were transferred to shelving which had been constructed in the stone rooms, and then sorted out by experts according to their special needs. After this, the books were removed from their bindings and taken to the heating plant of the railroad station. Every resource had to be made use of, as the need arose, and the ingenuity of those

57

Florentines and soldiers loading ancient books on a truck at the side entrance
of the Biblioteca Nazionale

working to salvage the books was outstanding. At the railway station heating plant, the separated pages were individually washed, pressed and dried out by teams of young students. The dangers seemed endless; there was fear of development of mold, worries that the pages might become brittle after drying, but each problem was met with intelligence and resourcefulness. After drying out at the railway station, the books were returned to Fort Belvedere, where they were treated with thymol crystals to prevent mildew. From there, they were to be dispatched to the National Library for the final restoration.

5

Appeal for Volunteers

The State Archives, one of the richest and most extensive in Europe, are housed in a building attached to the Uffizi, right along the river. What happened at the Archives on the day of the flood and the period immediately afterward symbolizes what happened in the libraries, churches, and museums throughout the city.

The director of the Archives, Dr. Sergio Camerani, was trapped in his home the day of the flood. Finally, early on the morning of November 5th he was able to get through the barrier of water and head for the Archives. As he made his way through the mud, past demolished shops and crumbled cars, he was terrified at the thought of what he might find. The Archives contained all the invaluable documents of Florentine and Tuscan history. In its five hundred rooms and on its forty-five miles of shelves were, among many other things, an extremely rare collection of diplomatic documents on parchment: about 150,000 single items, many of which dated to the year 1000; fascinating records of the Medici family who ruled Florence; letters of Machiavelli and of the painter Piero della Francesca; all in all, material that is constantly being consulted by scholars from all over the world, essential to the study of European history.

When Camerani arrived, he was greeted by a small group of people who had arrived there before him; among them were two who lived on the ground floor of the Archives. The flood had taken them completely by surprise. They had saved themselves and their families, but they had lost everything else. It was impossible to know just yet

Carrying what little they could salvage from their homes, Florentines wander through the streets in search of lodging

what had happened to the Archives. The entire ground floor had been submerged, thousands and thousands of volumes and files of documents were buried in mud. An enormous chasm produced by the collapse of a vault was dramatic evidence of the unprecedented catastrophe.

The small group made their way through the rubble into the Archives itself. Camerani felt a wave of helplessness overcome him, confronted as he was (he learned later) by forty large rooms, a total of 45,000 volumes, almost four miles of shelving buried in mud. How could they begin, what could they do? They were just a small group of elderly people, most of whom were worried about their own homes and possessions and families, with no equipment at their disposal.

It seemed hopeless until someone suggested a radio appeal for volunteers to carry out the enormous task of salvation. "I was very skeptical," Camerani has written in a moving article on those first heroic days, published in the Italian magazine *Nuova Antologia* in June, 1967. "That there were people ready to carry provisions, to try to save people and possessions, to clear out streets and houses, yes, but that we could find people prepared to throw themselves into the mud to save what for the general public were only old, useless bits of paper, good to pass the time for those with nothing better to do —well, I didn't believe it. But I had no other choice, and so I took up the suggestion."

The following afternoon, Camerani's appeal was transmitted on the radio—along with countless other appeals for aid and recommendations for sanitary precautions. He was still skeptical.

But the director of the State Archives was mistaken. To his astonishment, the entrance to the Archives was crammed full of people the next morning. There were people of all kinds and all ages, ready and willing to do whatever they could. There was a group of young Americans studying in Florence, organized by their professors, who accompanied them; there were German students, French students, English students, a Japanese student. There were Italians of all ages—lawyers, professors, distinguished gentlemen with gray hair, and, above all, students. Some were repaying a debt they owed to the Archives which had served them in their scholarly researches; others were instinctively aware of their importance to the cultural heritage of the world.

"They came noisily up the staircases in groups of eight or ten at a time," says Camerani. "Girls with flowing hair in slacks and boots, hippies with long hair and beards, children of eleven or twelve, elegant young men whose suits were destined for a certain and glorious end, presented themselves at the entrance with high-spirited self-confidence and the knowledge that they were needed, asking only: What is to be done? Where does one begin?"

It was then that the chains were organized, columns of students, climbing up the narrow winding staircase from the basement to the upper floors of the Archives. The stronger students went to the basement; in order to make a pathway, they removed tons of mud by means of buckets which were then emptied in the courtyards of the building. Once the basement was accessible, the students would penetrate into the darkness and fish for the slime-covered volumes of documents. One by one these large volumes, dripping with filth, were passed from student to student, from the basement up to the higher floors.

Between sixty and eighty students formed each of these chains which wound up the long staircases, through the cold, damp narrow corridors of the old palace. At the end were dilapidated, primitive handcarts into which the documents were piled and transferred to other rooms to be spread out. For several days, three of these chains functioned simultaneously from different points in the Archives to carry the precious volumes from the damp, mud-covered basement.

"Then there began for the State Archives," writes Camerani, "what without exaggeration could be called the strangest days in all its more than one hundred years of existence." To Dr. Sergio Camerani, who had up to then concerned himself with formal arrangements, inquiries from scholars, inventories, and above all administrative and bureaucratic matters, new and urgent problems presented themselves. "Those who had answered my appeal for volun-

Italian and foreign students work to save precious historical books

*In the State Archives building,
the flood destroyed the cellar
and first floor of the building*

teers had asked for nothing," says Camerani, "only to work, but just for this reason, and because their work was carried on in such appalling conditions, immersed in the dampness, exposed to bitterly cold drafts from nine in the morning until the last glimmer of light late in the afternoon, it was necessary at least to guarantee them a little nourishment. It was the least one could do. But how could all these people—most of them endowed with formidable appetites—be provided for?"

A director from the Archives went to the food distribution center which had been set up at the stadium and was given the necessary food. In addition, food was arriving from other sources, and the problem became one of handing out the food to the volunteers. For this the austere, imposing entrance hall of the State Archives underwent a radical transformation. Huge tables were arranged in an L shape; behind them, women and less able-bodied men spent hours running an improvised cafeteria—opening cans, slicing salami, cutting bread, fixing sandwiches. At noon, the mobs of hungry, tired workers would assault the food, and for an hour the task of handing out sandwiches, milk, mineral water, chocolate—anything available—would continue. Then the weary volunteers would carry their "lunch" to other rooms, sprawl out on the damp floors, or on sacks of sawdust, and eat amidst the almost overwhelming stench of mud and fuel oil. But no one complained; the food was eaten with the same enthusiasm with which the filthy documents were being rescued.

In addition to feeding these volunteers, it was necessary to watch out for their health in these unsanitary conditions. One morning Camerani entered his office to find himself face to face with a young man in a white uniform who informed him that he was a medical student, anxious to help as best he could. With this beginning, the huge, impressive reading room was transformed into an infirmary. Where a few days before there had been precious documents in Italian history, there were now basins, sterilizers, bandages, alcohol and anti-tetanus and anti-typhus serums. A doctor from a neighboring town took charge; each morning, after having disinfected

Mud-spattered volunteers on Piazza della Signoria. In the background is Cellini's bronze statue of Perseus in the Loggia dei Lanz

Student volunteers from Padua on Piazza Santa Croce during lunch break

wounds, injected serums and handed out vitamins, he seated himself at one of the tables that had previously held the correspondence of Niccolo Machiavelli and the letters of Lorenzo the Magnificent and chewed a salami sandwich, while drinking a glass of wine.

"In those chaotic days," says Camerani, "I had divided the volunteers, in my mind, into two groups—the excitable and the calm. The former were the 'diggers,' those engaged in recovering the documents, who formed the chains. Boisterous, shouting, always ready for a joke, they had to pause often from their exhausting work. They needed some strength, and so regular distributions of brandy were made, but they had their own way of keeping up their morale. I learned one day that a strictly alternating chain had been formed: young man, young girl, young man, young girl, etc., who passed volumes, together with a kiss. And there was not one of the older generation who dared to protest, from a feeling of affectionate indulgence tinged not a little with nostalgic envy.

"The calm group was to be found in another wing of the building, on the second floor. The putrid books arrived up there, and a large band of elderly gentlemen, distinguished ladies, and young people of all sorts who did not feel up to braving the chains, took one each and, seated at improvised tables, with infinite patience began to separate the pages one by one and interleave them with absorbent paper. In the first days, the interleavers amused themselves by devising the best way of separating the pages: with paper-knives, little plastic calenders, or some other object. Then they tried deciphering a few words—a fifteenth-century letter, an eighteenth-century scrawl. But it was still tedious work. Then someone took the risk of bringing in a small radio, and since no one complained, the example was followed by others. Soon through the spacious rooms carpeted with invaluable manuscripts were heard the notes of the latest songs. Some volunteers beat time with their feet, and others sang under their breath, while a young man with a supermarket cart went from table to table calling out, 'Who wants absorbent paper?' since he had been honored with the job of supplying it."

*Florentine students work
to save valuable historical
books in the State Archives*

Looking back on those frantic, exciting days of dedication, Dr. Camerani unhesitatingly acknowledges his debt to the young people of Florence and of the world. Years of restoration work remain, and it will be a difficult period. But a large part of the State Archives will eventually be recovered. "Without the help of the volunteers, above all of the young people with their ardent enthusiasm and energy, the immense amount of material submerged by the flood would have remained for months and months under the mud and would have been irremediably lost. Instead, within three weeks or a little more, everything had been recovered. The heroic days of the Archives are over; there only remains the memory of the tumultuous, dramatic period, illuminated by the unlooked-for, spontaneous contribution of those very young people whom we older people have always regarded with little faith."

6

City in Chaos

While the valiant rescue operations went on in Florence's churches, museums and libraries, it was also essential to feed and clothe the people. It is impossible to imagine the chaos that reigned in Florence those first days after the flood. In a sense, each part of the city had to act as a separate unit, its inhabitants taking care of each other by whatever limited means were at their disposal. There was practically no food, entire families were without clothing; thousands, having lost all, were homeless. The spirit of the people was extraordinary. Whatever food and clothing was brought in from non-flooded areas by friends was shared. Private citizens were assuming public responsibilities.

In San Niccolò, Maria Luigia Guaita, Nello Pratolini, and their neighbors talked from window to window and when it was time to eat, food was passed by rope from window sill to window sill. Food, too, arrived from the hills above, passed from street to street and house to house by any means possible. By Sunday morning, a truck, led by a neighborhood parish priest, was able to make its way through the mud; on it were bread, mineral water, milk, and sugar which were first given to the children. Throughout most of the city, these scenes were repeated.

A major problem those first days was the organization of the distribution of food and clothing. Thousands of Florentines had been driven from their homes, or seen their clothing and food destroyed; a large percentage of food stores had been devastated by the flood, and the supplies were strictly limited. In charge of the general operation of food and clothing distribution was the Prefettura—a local government organization, which controls the department of welfare. Most of the city's inhabitants relied upon supplies from the towns near Florence that had been spared from the flood—Bologna, Pistoia, Massa, and others. But trucks full of food and clothing also began to arrive from all over Italy and from the rest of Europe, from neighboring countries such as France and Switzerland. To handle all of this it was decided to set up one large central distribution point at the huge, modern football stadium which lies on the edge of the city, an area that had not been flooded. From the stadium, food and clothing would be dispatched throughout the city by trucks and buses. In that way, the needy would be provided for. Soon, however, it became clear that this system did not work. A truck laden with food would stop in a square or on a street corner, would distribute the food and go away. But there was no prior announcement of the truck's arrival, and hundreds of people half-buried in their cellars digging out the mud and slime remained below, unaware that food was being distributed up above. To reach all the people, a further step was taken: local centers, in the most severely flooded areas, were set up to distribute the food and clothing. By this method, everyone in the neighborhood would know just where to go for help.

This too was not ideal; the aged and sick could not leave their homes, and people with young children were afraid to bring them into the street or to leave them in the damp-infested apartments alone. Each man had to look out for himself and for his neighbor as well. Rules and regulations could serve as a guide to behavior, but no more than that. There had to be among the Florentines an atmosphere of understanding, born from one common idea: need. And this overall concept of need had to function above all in the main distribution center at the stadium to which requests were made, either by telephone or in person, from the various local centers.

The central distribution center was largely manned by officials

A Florentine resident, overcome with grief and fatigue

*Soldiers and civilians
work to dig the city out
of the mud*

*Some of the victims who have
received aid.
In the background is the Loggia
in the Piazza della Signoria*

of the Prefettura, an organization notoriously bogged down by rules and formalities. Requests had to be formally written down, supplies given away carefully noted, lists made in duplicate, and so on. But even among this "official" group, there were human beings who felt for the people and their needs, who were willing to break rules and depart from inhuman formulae. Among these was Vittoria de Pasquale, a fiery, proud Florentine who had fought hard against the Fascists in World War II and who, within the food distribution center, was again ready to fight as a human being, not as a machine, for the welfare of the Florentines.

"Our orders," said Signora de Pasquale, "were to give food only to representatives of the local centers, not to individuals. How could I possibly obey this rule? I saw people coming in, covered with mud, hungry, exhausted. Could I refuse them? They were hungry, so I gave them food."

One afternoon, an official from the State Archives came to the center in his car. The three hundred volunteers who were working to clean out the Archives, from early morning to evening, had no food. The representative from the Archives was told to fill out a form for each volunteer receiving food—three hundred requisition forms! Fortunately Vittoria de Pasquale was nearby and overheard the conversation. Without a word, she began loading the man's car with bread, cheese, biscuits, mineral water, brandy, and chocolate—anything she could find. And no forms were filled out. The man from the State Archives went away reassured that human beings were indeed working within the system.

"But we can't give indiscriminately to everyone," was the official cry to which Signora de Pasquale could only reply that it was better to risk giving to the wrong people than not giving to the right.

Day after day, a handful of Florentines worked around the clock, sometimes as many as twenty-two hours at a stretch, to feed the hungry, driven on by the single principle of need. One night, a police car drove up to the stadium, carrying a pathetic, shivering man, his clothes soaked through, his teeth chattering. The policeman explained that the man

76

*Individuals like
Vittoria de Pasquale had to
assume public responsibility*

*(Next page)
Soldiers splash through
the streets carrying their
sad burdens
—the dead and the living*

had lost everything, didn't know where his family was, and had fallen into such despair that he tried to throw himself in the Arno. Compassion in such a case had to be substituted for forms; there were no rules to be applied. The desperate man was given dry clothing, some hot milk and brandy, and, above all, some hope: instead of dying in the mud, he believed it was necessary to make something new grow from it.

The function at the stadium center was to distribute food; another center had been set up for clothing. But here too rules had to be overlooked. To the food distribution center would come many people with shoes and shirts and overcoats and suits and dresses. To turn these gifts over to another center seemed absurd. The people who came for food in their mud-soaked clothing could use these gifts of warm sweaters, coats, and children's clothing. So, on their own initiative, the small group at the stadium set up a private center for the distribution of clothing.

Children in rags, alone; a pregnant woman whose husband was busy digging out their few possessions from the mud; the desperate—these were the people that Vittoria de Pasquale and the others tried to help, not as part of the government machine but as human beings responding to other human beings. "I tried to take care of individuals," Signora de Pasquale explained, "because it was a more direct way of helping people, of showing that we weren't government administrators, but *people* who understood and wanted to help and be near them. My job, as much as giving out food and clothing, was to give these people courage. You could see after a few days that they were beginning to grow weary, and that their dignity was beginning to give way in the struggle with need, with fatigue, with all kinds of problems, the filth that surrounded them and the sense of isolation in their struggle. In the last analysis, every Florentine was on his own, especially in the beginning. In those first days, the people felt there was no government or anyone to assume the responsibility, the weight of this tragedy. Everyone had to make it on his own. This was something I could understand, beyond the drama of the flood itself, this feeling that

81

(Top) Hundreds of Florentines wait in line to receive food at the Piazza della Signoria. In the foreground is Bandinelli's Hercules *(Bottom) People try to salvage some of their belongings*

we were alone. I wanted to make these people realize that someone *was* thinking of them."

It was a time for action and comprehension. Those people helping strangers as well as neighbors neither wanted nor expected gratitude. They were doing a duty, fulfilling a responsibility. One evening a young man in torn clothing came to the center and timidly asked for food. After he had explained to Signora de Pasquale that he lived in one of the hardest-hit sections of the city, she filled his arms with everything in sight. As he started to leave, he turned to her and, even more shyly, asked if he might have something with which to cover his mother, explaining that their home had been ruined, that his mother couldn't sleep at night because of the cold and damp. Without a word from his benefactor, he was given not only blankets but an armful of warm clothing for his mother—and for himself. Overwhelmed with gratitude, he grabbed Signora de Pasquale's two hands and kissed them. "Don't be silly," she said. "I'm not a bishop. But when things are better for you and life has begun again, try to come around and tell me what happened. I'll be happy to see you."

When not working at the center, the small group of workers would visit hard-hit sections of the city, trying to take stock of the general situation themselves. One day fifty chickens arrived from a neighboring community. Having heard that conditions at the psychiatric hospital were particularly bad, Signora de Pasquale found a car to take her out there with the chickens. It was night time when she arrived; outside the hospital were mud-covered mattresses, and from inside the building came the screams of the terrified patients. The hospital seemed to stand in isolation, dark and abandoned amidst the unlighted streets, the only signs of life being those screams from within. The doors were all open, but the gates were barred to prevent the patients from escaping. Signora de Pasquale and the driver of the car stood in front shouting, but no one came. So, up to their knees in mud, climbing over some boards that had been put down to make access to the hospital possible, they entered. The wards and clinic were in ruins, covered with mud; beds were on the floor. Finally, a harassed nurse

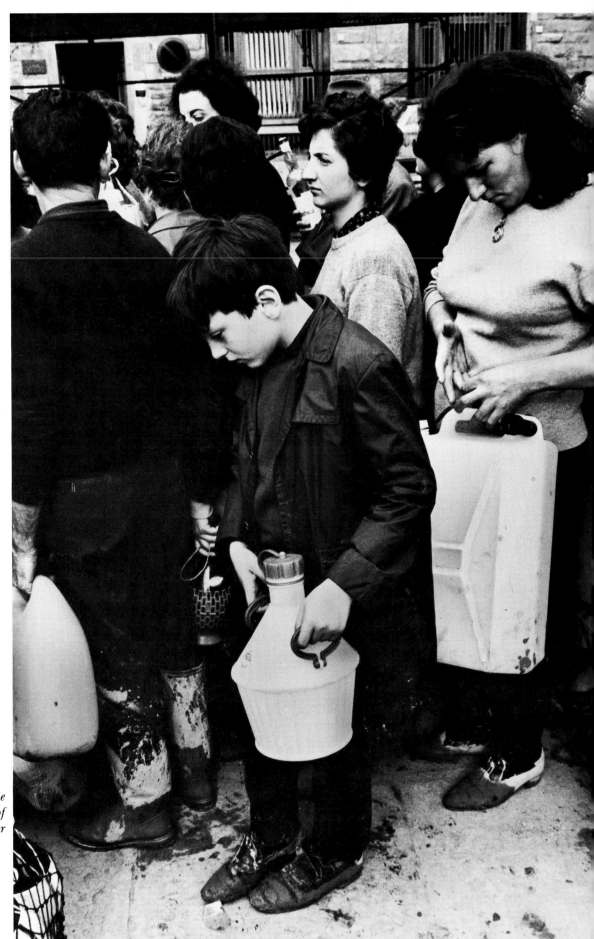

*Florentines wait in line
for distribution of
food and water*

appeared and gratefully took the chickens. It was a horrifying experience, dramatically illustrating the need to continue the fight to feed Florence.

It was, for Vittoria de Pasquale, a tragic period as it was for all of Florence. But it was not without its positive aspects, above all the dignity and unselfishness shown by so many of her fellow citizens. And something else, the spirit of the young people. "Groups of them, individuals, some very young, would come to the center and ask to be put to work, to carry, to unload, anything. The first day my own nephew Bernardo came begging me to put him to work, explaining that he just couldn't remain idle.

"So he took his family car and went to one of the worst districts, where the water had risen twenty feet, and he went into every open door, up the stairs where he found groups of old, sick, abandoned people, people who were physically unable to ask for help, who desperately needed food and clothing. He would come back to report to me, and I would send him out with a car full of supplies. Maybe some government official would have asked, "But who are these people, their names, can you be sure they need and are entitled to the food?"

7

A Dying Masterpiece

At seven in the morning of November 6th, a note, scrawled on the back of an envelope, was delivered to Dr. Umberto Baldini. It was signed by Dr. Ugo Procacci, and it read:

"I have been told that Cimabue's *Crucifix* is in danger; it seems that the head and body are already seriously damaged. Leave all other work and come immediately to Santa Croce."

Later, in a symposium on the causes of the Florence flood, Baldini described those awful hours. "That note," he wrote, "had been brought to me by a young student whose name I still do not know, though I shall never forget his bewildered expression and his anxious words, spoken breathlessly as if he had run a long race. The story he told me still sounds in my ears like a lament.

"That was the most dramatic moment of those memorable days. That brief message marked the culmination of the tragedy for me and for all of us."

Baldini rushed to the church of Santa Croce. It was true; one of the greatest treasures of Florence was dying. Giovanni Cimabue, a thirteenth-century master, has been called "the father of Florentine painting." Giorgio Vasari, the Renaissance biographer, called him a man "born to give the first light to the art of painting." His *Crucifix*, portraying the agony of Christ, was painted between 1280 and 1285. It had already survived a series of disasters, including the floods of 1333 and 1466, survived because it had been placed high in the church of Santa Croce. It barely escaped damage in 1512, when a violent storm

*Interior of Santa Croce.
The photo shows the height
which the flood reached*

*The ruined interior of
Santa Croce, covered with
water and mud*

caused a mass of debris to fall on the spot where it had formerly been placed. In later years it was moved in and out of various chapels; and finally to the top floor of the Uffizi galley. Only two years before the flood it had been returned to Santa Croce and put in its low-lying museum.

This time the large crucifix had been submerged to the top of the head of Christ. When the water withdrew, blisters appeared on the surface; the wood had contracted too quickly and the layer of color could not adjust itself. The paint was flaking away. When Baldini arrived, the face and body of Christ were almost completely gone. The flesh looked as though it had been destroyed by an explosion, shriveled and swollen as if it had been burned, and hanging in shreds that looked as if they might fall off at any moment.

"The men who were with me did not speak," Baldini says. "They looked at me, waiting, ready to begin work. But there was only silence. They did not hear my voice—they only saw tears on my face (the first I shed), just as they were to see tears a little later on Procacci's pale face, when he came back a second time. . . . It was the students who broke the silence: 'If you cry,' one of them said to me, 'what are we to do?' " So it was that the job of removing the battered painting from its position had to begin.

The enormous weight of the crucifix made it difficult to move from its vertical position, but the "descent" of the cross began. For seven hours, Baldini and his helpers labored with the tools and materials at hand. Even a tea strainer was used to sieve the mud in the vain hope of being able to recover a few scraps of paint flakes in the area around the base.

For days, the monks at Santa Croce sifted the mud to find further pieces of color belonging to Cimabue's masterpiece. But this great Florentine treasure was eighty per cent ruined. This includes almost the entire body of Christ, for the paint used there seems to have been the most vulnerable. This great painting which Dr. Procacci has called "one of the hinges of Italian art," can never be restored. Its loss is a great and immeasurable tragedy. "It's a corpse," said Professor Freder-

At an intersection, streaks on the building and sign show the high water mark of the flood

Cimabue's Crucifix,
before the flood

(Right) after the flood

ick Hartt of the University of Pennsylvania, when he saw it. "And it can only be displayed as a relic."

Indeed, it seems probable that the Crucifix will be rehung in its tragic state next to a photograph of the original, as a bitter reminder of the day in November when the waters ravaged Florence.

With that, a period somehow came to an end. During those first heroic days, the people of Florence had little time to think—there was too much to do. They had been carried along on a wave of enthusiasm and dedication which allowed no time for reflection. They had been busy responding to an emergency, and their response had been both courageous and energetic. But now it was time to count the tragic losses, and to restore somehow the city of Florence.

8

The World Responds

As word spread throughout Florence that the beloved Cimabue *Crucifix* was dying, so word spread throughout the world that the very life of Florence was threatened. A cultural heritage which all civilized mankind held in common was in danger.

With how many millions of people throughout its history had this jewellike city shared its unique beauties. It had been a source of joy and a fountain of knowledge for the countless visitors that came to it year after year; it had been a special kind of haven, a place of inspiration for some of the greatest literary figures of all time. The great French satirist, Francois Rabelais, author of *Gargantua and Pantagruel*, had visited there in 1535; so had the brilliant essayist, Michel de Montaigne in 1580. In 1803, the French Romantic novelist François René de Chateaubriand drew inspiration from Florence as did, in later years, other important French writers such as Anatole France and Alexandre Dumas. One of the greatest of all novels, Dostoevski's *The Idiot*, was written in Florence in 1868 and 1869. A modern Russian writer, Boris Pasternak, spent a happy period of his life there. The German poet, Rainer Maria Rilke, lived there in 1898.

Florence had played a constructive role in the life and work of many American writers too. Among those who visited there were Mark Twain; Henry Wadsworth Longfellow, who translated Dante's *Divine Comedy*; Nathaniel Hawthorne, who wrote his novel *The Marble Faun* in Florence; and Sinclair Lewis, who spent the last years of his life in his home on a hill above the Arno.

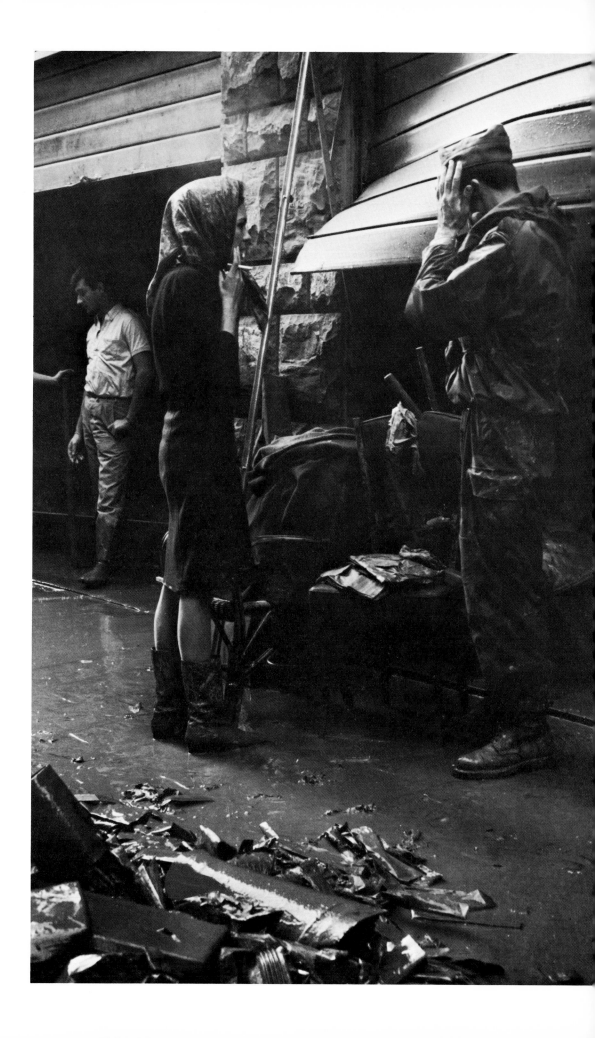

While Florence has meant something special to people of many nations, perhaps no foreigners have been more deeply attached to it than have the English. Florence Nightingale was born there in 1823. Elizabeth Barrett Browning lived there for many years, until her death in 1861.

In Florence Robert Browning wrote *The Ring and the Book,* and Percy Bysshe Shelley wrote *Ode to the West Wind.* John Milton had been in Florence between 1638 and 1639, and Byron deeply admired the city. Other English writers who paid lengthy visits or took up residence in Florence include Frances Trollope, Thomas Hardy, George Eliot, Charles Dickens, D. H. Lawrence, W. Somerset Maugham, and Aldous Huxley.

The city had honored these authors and their works by putting up plaques throughout the town to commemorate their visits and sojourns in Florence. Now it was time for the world to honor Florence, the great Renaissance city that could no longer be taken for granted. "Florence," Richard Burton was to say in a film he later made to aid the Florentines and their city, "belongs to the world."

And the world responded, generously and in a rare spirit of unity and international co-operation. It would take volumes to enumerate the kinds of aid and the methods by which it arrived from all over the globe, but a very incomplete list will give an idea of the scope of it. First, there were the immediate needs to be filled. Truckloads of food and clothing rolled in from other Italian cities, from Austria and Switzerland, from France and Germany. Urgently needed driers arrived from Munich, and pumps were sent from Indiana. The United States Army dispatched food, clothing, vehicles of all kinds, generators, and even prefabricated housing units. From England came three thousand blankets, powdered milk and 50,000 doses of vaccine to prevent the much-feared spread of disease throughout the city. From Scotland came water pumps, blankets, and medicines. From Holland engineers arrived with water-decontamination equipment, and from Genoa came frogmen who dove to the river's depths in an attempt to recover valuable drowned property. From Russia came flood-relief aid estimated

*A young girl beginning
the restoration
of an ancient volume*

Passing damaged volumes from hand to hand along the human chain of rescuers

The pages of the books are first washed in plain water

at more than a half a million dollars, and Israel offered to take in more than one hundred Florentine children to vacation in its kibbutzim, or co-operative communities.

Perhaps the most moving gift of all came from the town of Aberfam in Wales. It was a gift of toys and clothing which had belonged to the small children who had not too long before lost their lives in a tragic landslide.

When the waters had receded, and most of the mud was cleared away, it was time to think of the specific needs in restoring the art of Florence, its museums and churches. Experts from all parts of the world began to arrive—from London's Victoria and Albert Museum, from Paris's Louvre, and from many American museums and universities. Restorers came to the city in large numbers from Czechoslovakia, Greece, Poland, America, Russia, Scandinavia, England, Austria, France, and Germany.

Organizations were speedily formed throughout the world to come to the aid of the stricken city, in every aspect of its grief. One group, the British Society for the Protection of Animals, even raised money for the animals of Florence. Collaboration among these rescue funds, museums, and libraries and among restorers of many nations was remarkable. Some countries undertook specific projects: the French were to be responsible for the restoration of a church, Santa Maria Maddalena dei Pazzi; the English were in charge of the Horne Museum; the Dutch looked after the restoration of the Casa Buonarotti.

The British, in recognition of the special place Florence holds in their country, contributed generously through a number of organizations, among them the British Consulate in Florence Fund, Lord Hastings' Italian People's Flood Appeal, and the British Italian Society.

The United States, too, responded quickly to the appeal for aid, largely through the creation of the Committee to Rescue Italian Art (CRIA). With Mrs. John F. Kennedy as Honorary President and under the leadership of Professor Bates Lowry of Brown University, this organization has played a significant part in the recovery of Florence. A very few days after the flood, two American professors, Frederick

Hartt of the University of Pennsylvania and Fred S. Licht of Brown University, flew to Florence. There they secured precise information on the extent of the crisis and the needs of the city's museums and churches. They established direct contact with Professor Myron Gilmore, director at the time of Harvard's Center for Renaissance Studies at I Tatti, a superb villa just outside of Florence. I Tatti was the home of Bernard Berenson, an American and the greatest connoisseur of Renaissance art of this century. At his magnificent villa, Berenson had built an incomparable library and collection of Renaissance paintings which, upon his death in 1959, he left to Harvard University. For a while after the flood, this American-owned villa became the center to which most Florentine cultural institutions turned for help during the crisis. As the Committee to Rescue Italian Art raised close to two and a half million dollars in the United States, Professor Gilmore and his co-workers at I Tatti oversaw the distribution of CRIA-donated supplies, initiated consultation with Italian authorities, planned periodic inspection trips to damaged churches, libraries, and museums, and arranged for the American restorers to inspect the damage and to take part in the rescue work. In the course of CRIA's three-year program, it will continue to supply funds, equipment, and personnel; it has made and will continue to make an inestimable contribution to the recovery of Florence.

On a larger, international scale, UNESCO (United Nations Educational, Scientific and Cultural Organization) has come to the aid of Florence, its members responding to an eloquent plea by René Maheu, the Director-General, which read in part:

"Florence bemired, it is the springtime of our hearts which is forever disfigured. We will not resign ourselves to such disasters . . . .

"I am sure that once again mankind will not fail to acknowledge and act to save its common heritage, thereby acknowledging again and reaffirming its profound spiritual unity.

"Each one of us knows himself to be a member of the Family of Man. How then could any one of us remain indifferent to the fate of these most precious jewels in our common heritage?"

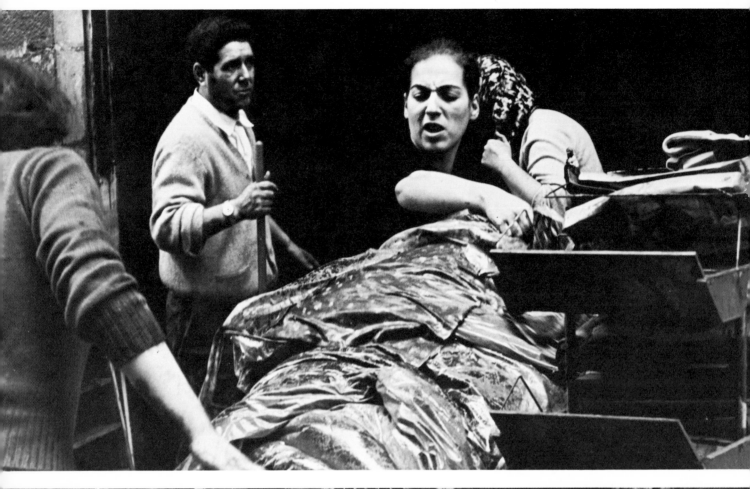

The world did not remain indifferent; it responded to the needs of a great city in crisis.

The response of the world—through its experts and its organizations—was gratifying in every way, but the most heartening aspect of those first weeks after the flood was the response of the young people to this unprecedented disaster.

No one will ever know where they all came from; no one has a complete list of their names and nationalities, but suddenly the Florentines saw them spring up from all sides, a friendly army without uniform, whose weapons were pails and shovels and—most important— determination. They began to arrive in the stricken areas on the morning of November 5th. The Florentines among them had seen their own homes thrown into confusion, their younger sisters and brothers often without milk or bread, and yet they came spontaneously, without waiting to be called. They were soon joined by fellow students from all parts of the world, joined in the battle to save the people and the books and the works of art of the wounded city of Florence. They reported to no one—they knew they were needed, and they instinctively went where they felt the need to be the greatest, and they set to work. Hundreds, then thousands of young students fought with the same passion in the libraries and museums as in the mud-filled doorways and basements of the poorer homes and in the devastated stores. They shoveled the mud, repaired wiring, fixed plumbing. They ran through the town, sounding the alarm, recruiting more volunteers. They fought their way through the mud and debris in search of cotton and of Kleenex, essential in those first days to prevent further damage to the masterpieces whose lives were threatened by the flood. Day and night they worked under difficult and often dangerous conditions, moving the old and sick to safety just as they passed along the books and paintings to the upper floors of libraries and museums. They made no distinction between men and books—to help each was a part of the same moral obligation. Both were acts of respect towards mankind. The older people of Florence watched them with gratitude and admiration; without their un-

Homeless people and their ruined possessions

Italian soldier hastens drying process with electric heater as students work on damaged books at Biblioteca Nazionale

Plaque outside Biblioteca Nazionale testifying to the city's gratitude to the students for their work after the flood

IN QVESTA BIBLIOTECA
E ALTROVE IN FIRENZE
DOVE L'ALLVVIONE DEL 4 NOVEMBRE 1966
PIV AVEVA IMPERVERSATO
NVMEROSI GIOVANI ITALIANI E STRANIERI
TRA L'ACQVA E IL FANGO
CON GENEROSA ABNEGAZIONE
RECARONO AIVTO

selfish help the disaster would have been many times greater.

They continued to pour into Florence from all over the world. There were long-haired *provos* from Amsterdam, hippies from London. Already in Florence were more than five hundred American students studying in those universities that had branches in Florence—Harvard, Smith, Syracuse, Gonzaga, Florida State, and Stanford. They struggled enthusiastically beside students from all parts of Italy, from Iraq and Canada, from Holland and from Switzerland. There were Israeli students from Jerusalem's Academy of Fine Arts, working alongside students from England and France. All political, social, and ideological differences were forgotten. Florence had to be saved, and Florence belonged to all of them, whatever else they believed or wherever they came from. If their special attention was turned to saving books, it is because to these students, books are the most highly valued treasures. By rescuing the hundreds of thousands of volumes, they were saving not only an element of culture essential to their own personal studies, but an essential means of enrichment, of comprehension of both the past and the present. Never has man's respect for the written word been more dramatically demonstrated than in the affectionate tenacity these young people displayed in the struggle to save the libraries of Florence.

A young university student from Florence, Tommaso Detti, expressed the feelings of these unselfish young people. "We students, Italians and foreigners, worked to help individuals, but above all to save the cultural patrimony. It was all spontaneous; we just went where we were needed and dug in. The students worked everywhere—in the libraries and in the museums, and in the streets too. I was working at the Nazionale while my brother was shovelling mud off a bridge. Maybe there wasn't much organization, and maybe we were even responsible for further damage in some cases—we didn't know that a flooded book had to be handled in a particular way. Anyway, later on there was some organization, and groups of us were sent where we were especially needed. But on the whole it remained spontaneous. After working at the Nazionale for a few days, I went to help a friend clear her house of mud and debris. Some afternoons I'd help my brother dump loads from the trucks into the river. This turned out to be a mistake because it obstructed the river, but we didn't know: no one had told us where to dump the debris."

Governmental authority did indeed seem to be missing those first days, and the young people showed remarkable resourcefulness.

At one point there were more than three thousand students who had come to Florence to work, and finding places for them to sleep became a problem. For a while, they had slept on the ground, in doorways, a few feet away from the mud-infested basements. But sanitary conditions were dangerous, and the threat of disease serious. Rooms were impossible to find in a city where more than three-quarters of all hotels and boarding houses had been gutted by the flood, so unusual solutions had to be found—and were. A large number of the girls were quartered in the convents in and around Florence, and the boys were permitted to use railway cars as their dormitories. Since space was still limited, they slept in turns, and very short ones at that.

These young people had not come to Florence for comfort or for rest. They had come to save a city, and their very presence inspired hope and confidence among the people of Florence. These students helped to bring Florence back to life; they also demonstrated an inner strength, a sense of responsibility, and the courage to sustain a battle in which they wholeheartedly believed. No longer would their elders say they were living lives without meaning, no longer could it be said that they were nihilistic, believing in nothing. When put to the test, these members of the new generation proved themselves worthy in every respect. The grateful citizens of Florence called them "angels of the mud."

Outside the National Library of Florence, a plaque has been put up which reads: "In this library and elsewhere in Florence where the flood of November 4, 1966, most savagely raged, numerous young Italians and foreigners unselfishly came to the rescue through the water and the mud." This is a fitting commemoration of their work, as the eventual recovery of Florence will be a splendid tribute to their efforts.

9

A Miracle of Recovery

On November 27th, 1966, there occurred one of the first of what many have called the "miracles" of the recovery of Florence. The miracle of November 27th, as the reopening of the Teatro Comunale, Florence's opera house, has been called, was a man-made miracle, due to no supernatural forces. It was the result of extraordinarily hard work by a group of determined people; it has been described by an official of the theater as an "act of angry will power."

Located near the river, the opera house had taken the full force of the flood. The entire orchestra floor had been submerged, the seats coated with mud and oil, the curtain ravaged as if by a cyclone, the walls covered with what seemed to be an ugly black and yellow coat of paint, and the entire electrical system destroyed.

On the day following the flood, the Florence newspaper reported that the theater could not possibly function for at least three or four months. But the newspaper had not taken into account the proud determination of those connected with the opera. To the rescue came members of the orchestra, dancers from the ballet, and personnel from every department—administrators to ushers. They transformed themselves into angry shovelers, clearing the mud and debris from the theater.

Through their efforts, the opera season began a mere twenty-three days after the flood—only two days behind the original schedule. It was an emotional audience that filled the opera house on the night of the reopening. As they passed through the lobby, the people's attention

A view of the Teatro Comunale on November 27, 1966. On stage are all the people who made the opening of the opera season on that day possible

was called to souvenirs of those terrible days; there were photos of the wrecked theater and, in showcases, dramatic reminders of the damage done. On exhibition were two barely recognizable pianos, warped and discolored, as well as other smashed and splintered musical instruments of every kind. There were mud-encrusted tail coats and black trousers, for the basement of the buildings, where the instruments and musicians' clothing were kept, had been submerged.

Once in the theater, the audience was seated on seats lent by other theaters throughout Italy. Dampness still pervaded the walls, which showed a four-foot-high water line.

Before the actual performance began, there were speeches by those who helped make this "miracle" possible, and one official commented ironically that theirs was the only theater in the world with its own basement swimming pool.

The performance itself celebrated the 400th anniversary of one of Italy's greatest composers, Claudio Monteverdi, whose opera, *The Coronation of Poppea,* was sung. The cast wore costumes borrowed from Italy's greatest opera house, La Scala of Milan. They acted on boards of a stage that had been swollen with dampness, that had been repeatedly planed down, but had swelled again each evening, threatening the actors with their curved surfaces. But none of this mattered. The battle had been won, and the opera house had reopened.

By Christmas, the museums had reopened, if only as a symbolic gesture. Florence would recover, but it would be a long and costly struggle.

10

Miracles of Restoration

On December 22nd, 1967, little more than a year after the flood, an extraordinary and heartwarming exhibition opened on the ground floor of the National Museum, a museum that had itself been tragically damaged during the flood. The show was devoted to works that had already been restored since those terrible November days.

A great deal of attention centered on one object that for many symbolizes the city of Florence—a wooden model for the lantern that crowns the cathedral dome. Dominating the city is the great cathedral, topped by the superb dome that was designed by Filippo Brunelleschi, the first Renaissance architect and one of the greatest. On top of the dome is Brunelleschi's lantern, a light, decorative structure he was commissioned to design as the result of a competition held in 1436, and for which he constructed a delicate wooden model, itself an exquisite work of art. This model had been displayed on the ground floor of the Museum of the Cathedral; on the morning of the flood, the pressure of air and water exploded directly under Brunelleschi's model, shattering it and scattering its pieces in the mud and slime. An immediate search was made through the mud for the fragments of the precious model. Fortunately, because these small fragments did not remain in the water for too long and because cleaning was begun at once, the wooden model was almost completely salvaged. The pieces were gathered together and taken to a restoration laboratory in Bologna where, under controlled dehumidification, each was dried out and returned to its original form.

Each, then, was individually worked on and reinforced. Finally, with the use of a strong glue, the work was patched together. As it stood in its case in the center of the exhibition, Brunelleschi's model was again a symbol—this time of the recovery of the works of art of Florence, a tribute to the great skill and dedication of the people who would bring Florence back to life.

Most of the "miracles," as they were justifiably called, at the exhibition were the results of work done at a newly established restoration center, set up shortly after the flood in the fourteenth-century Palazzo Davanzati.

From the outside, the Palazzo Davanzati is a noble, majestic palace, one of the most distinguished in Florence. But inside—with the establishment, immediately after the flood, of the Restoration Center for Sculpture and the Minor Arts—it is a modern, up-to-date laboratory in which some of the finest smaller works of the museums and churches of Florence are being returned to their former states.

The Restoration Center is the result of a tremendous international effort to fulfill a need dramatized by the flood and its reckless damage to sculpture, wooden objects, arms, musical instruments, and textiles.

From the American Committee to Rescue Italian Art came the funds to equip the building itself for use (pressurized water, heat, lights, etc.), as well as funds to establish a restoration section for sculpture, a modern chemical laboratory, and an office. From the Italian National Research Council came funds for chemical research, and from the British Italian Art and Archives Rescue Fund, the money necessary to install and equip a modern laboratory for the restoration of wooden objects and armaments.

In charge of the research laboratory in the beginning was William Young, of the Boston Museum of Fine Arts, a man given much credit for the establishment and organization of the Center. From London's Victoria and Albert Museum came Kenneth Hempel, chief restorer of sculpture there. Both he and Mr. Young spent long hours training young Italian restorers to do the work on their own when necessary.

Top left) Brunelleschi's model for the lantern of the cathedral, before the flood;
Top right) Fragments from the model after recovery from the mud; (Middle) The
process of dehumidification; (Bottom) The model for the lantern, among other
restored works of art exhibited at the National Museum in December, 1967.

In the early days, these experts too supervised the work of young student volunteers who worked in the churches at the relatively simple, but painstaking job, of removing the fuel oil from the marble statues, for only the smaller works could be transferred to the laboratory. Both Young and Hempel returned to Florence often and regularly; they were assisted at various times by skilled restorers like Maddalena Saiko from Vienna, Kay Silberfield from Baltimore, and Angela Camargo from Mexico.

In the chemical laboratory, working closely with the restorers, were chemists from Italy, from Norway, and from England.

Restoration of wooden objects was supervised by men from Italy and Norway, aided by three young American students.

To work on restoration of ancient musical instruments, there came two German women—from Berlin and from Nuremburg—while five badly damaged instruments were sent to Holland for restoration; the necessary funds were raised in one evening by means of a benefit in a Dutch school.

A German expert arrived to supervise the restoration of armaments; he was assisted by a young Italian. And from Denmark came Dr. Kragh, a trained binder, to offer her services in the rebinding of the precious volumes damaged in the library of the National Museum.

In charge of the center is Dr. Cristina Piacenti Aschengreen, who efficiently weaves together the skills of her international team. For the work going on in the Palazzo Davanzati is truly an international effort. Experts from all over the world have unselfishly given of themselves, generously sharing the knowledge they have studied so many years to acquire. Abandoning professional jealousies, they have joined together in a fight to restore Florence's patrimony to its former glory.

Each room in the Davanzati bears witness to the skill of these dedicated technicians from all parts of the world, as they work to restore the masterpieces, many of which were given up as hopeless as they emerged from the mud and oily waters. Busts and sculptures, gilt Renaissance picture frames, inlaid furniture, stuccos, terra cottas, porcelain, ancient musical instruments, helmets and suits of armor—

(Top) In the Palazzo Davanzati, Mexican restorer Angela Camargo works on a tomb sculpture by Tino di Camaino, while in the foreground Italian restorer Giuglielmo Galli works on a marble bust (Below) Anne Boardman (left) and Anne Marie Ehrlich in the Palazzo Davanzati, working on busts from the top of the door to the chapel of San Luca

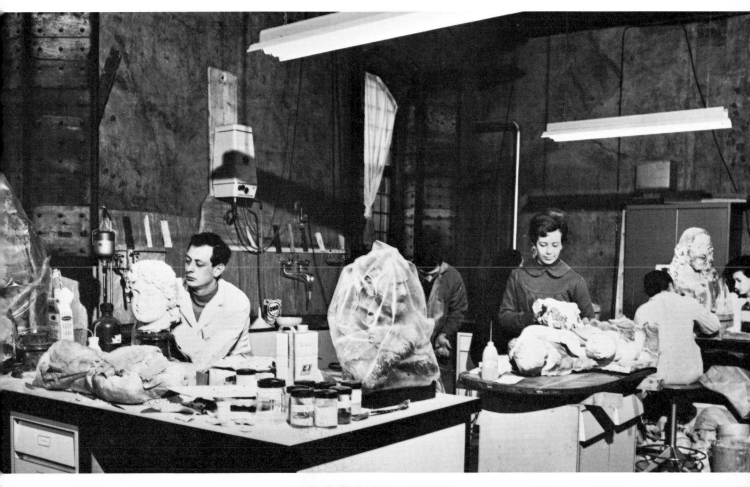
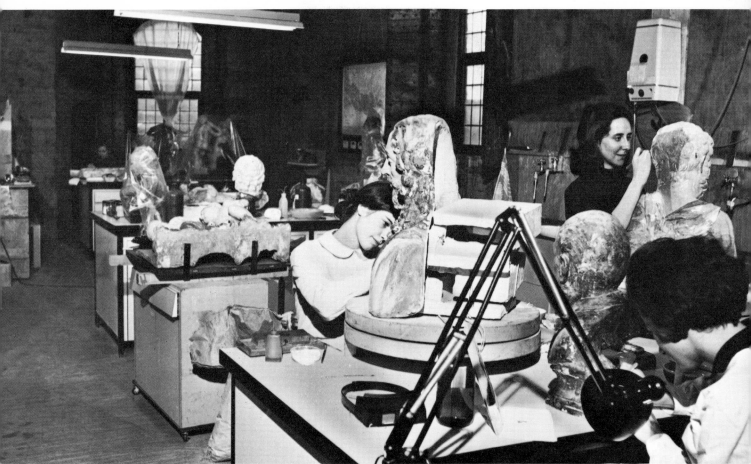

Fifteenth-century Florentine furniture after its recovery from the flood waters in the Horne Museum

The same piece after restoration by Giuliano Arretini

all are treated by specialists in separate departments of the Restoration Center. It is important that each object be treated individually, for there is no guarantee that any two objects, no matter how similar, would respond to the same treatment.

Two interesting examples are illustrated in the work being done on sculpture, so much of which was severely damaged by the flood waters. In one corner of the room devoted to restoration of marble sculpture sits Angela Camargo, a Mexican restorer, patiently working on the restoration of fragments of the tomb of Gastone della Torre, by Tino da Camaino, a fourteenth-century sculptor from Siena who specialized in sculptured tombs. These delicate marble sculptures had been found covered with slime in the crypt of Santa Croce after the flood, the harsh action of the water and dirt scratching the surface of the sculptures and causing them to crumble. To restore these sculptures to their former condition was a long and difficult project. First the dirt had to be removed by careful scraping with a spatula. The more deeply encrusted hard-to-remove dirt was then softened by the application of compresses of deionized water and sepiolite. Then, a mixture of sepiolite and a solvent was applied—the resultant mixture resembles an ordinary mud pack—to absorb the fuel oil and salts that were threatening the marble. When dried, this mixture was carefully removed with a spatula. Next the long job of consolidating the marble; this was accomplished by repeated application, by means of a small brush, of a polyvinyl acetate. Finally, using her hands in a kind of massage, Miss Camargo applied the patina of cosmoloid wax and the solvent.

Another room is dedicated to the delicate task of restoring wooden objects, wood having been most affected by the water and oil.

When the flood waters rushed through one of Florence's oldest churches, Sant' Ambrogio, reaching a level of almost eleven feet, they carried with them a painted wooden sculpture of Saint Sebastian, carved by Leonardo del Tasso in 1500. For eight days, the wooden figure, smashed into thirty pieces, lay in the mud and oily water. Among the many tasks during those first chaotic days of recovery, the salvage of

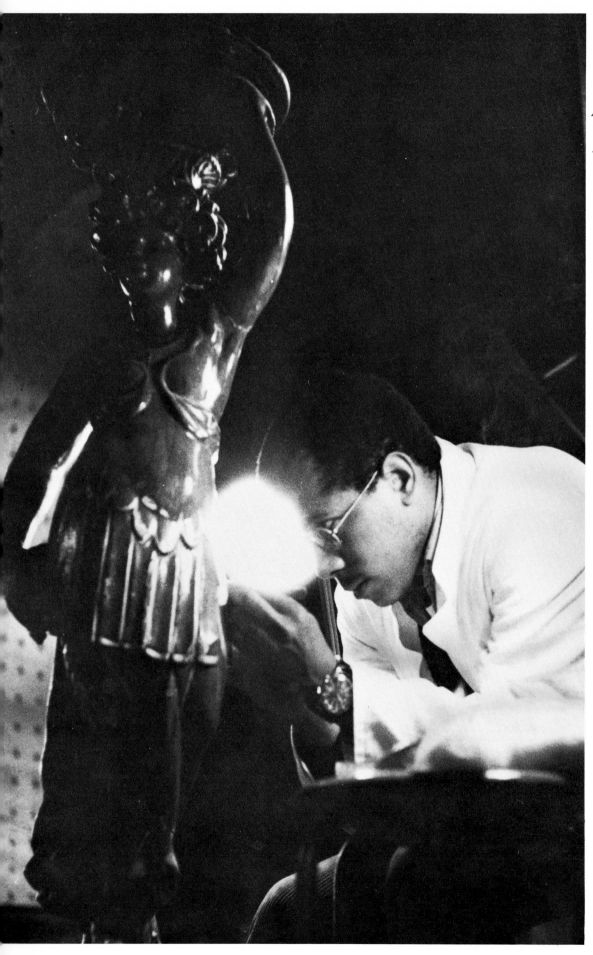

Among the American restorers was Ron Cunningham from New Jersey

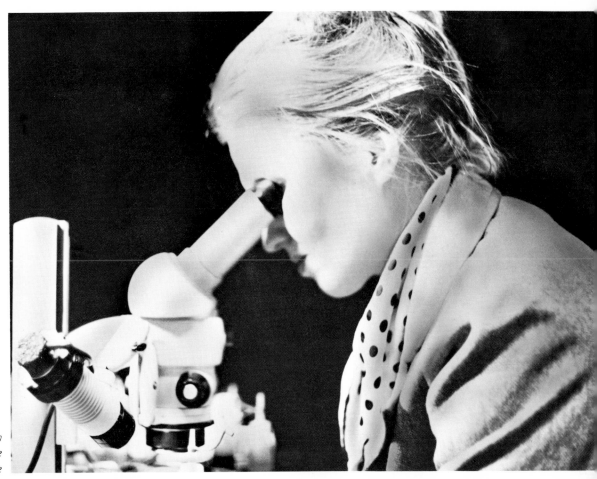

n Simonson Plather carefully examines cross sections of the paint through a microscope

Dr. Leif Einar Plather works on the wooden sculpture itself

wood sculpture received a relatively low priority. Nonetheless, due to the dedication of one man—Dr. Otello Caprara, a private restorer, who on his own initiative came daily from his home in Bologna to search among the mud and rubble—the thirty pieces of the painted wooden sculpture were gathered together one by one and taken to what used to be the kitchen of the Palazzo Davanzati, a room with humidity-control equipment. There the pieces dried, and the superficial oil was removed with cotton.

When it came time to begin the work of restoration, an expert was needed, a man who had had experience in the special field of restoration of painted wooden objects. Such a man was Dr. Leif Einar Plather of Norway, who worked in the National Gallery in Oslo. Ten days after the flood, Dr. Plather had come to Florence to see what kind of help was needed. After serious discussions with museum directors in Florence, it was decided that a number of Scandinavian restorers would be of use when the job of actual restoration could be put into operation. Soon the Scandinavian governments—Norway, Sweden, Denmark and Finland—through acts of parliament, pledged to supply a minimum of six restorers at a time for a period of three years to the city of Florence. The restorers would alternate, each serving one year, and so it was that Dr. Plather returned to Florence in July 1967. This time he came with his wife, Unn Simonson Plather, from Oslo's History Museum, a chemist who would also work in the Palazzo Davanzati.

Dr. Plather's assignment was restoration of the *Saint Sebastian*. Among his assistants was a young American, Ron Cunningham, a CRIA fellow who was studying for his doctorate at New York University's Institute of Fine Arts at the time of the flood. Ron had had experience in the United States, at the Rockefeller home in upper New York State, and in Egypt. This was a unique opportunity for further experience which would serve him well in his career as a conservator— that is, a restorer who is concerned with the preservation of paintings and sculpture as well as their restoration to their original state.

The recovery of Del Tasso's *Saint Sebastian* entailed complicated

Del Tasso's **Saint Sebastian**
before the flood

and difficult problems, calling for the skills of an expert restorer as well as an art historian. The first step was to examine the figure carefully, by means of photography as well as chemical analysis of a minuscule cross section of the paint to be examined through a microscope. Del Tasso's wood sculpture was painted a dark brown, but from the point of view of an art historian it was unlikely that such a work, created in 1500, would have been painted that color. Clues were gathered, and it was determined that under the dark brown, which was most probably painted on in the nineteenth century to make the figure appear bronze, there was a polychrome decoration. Microscopic examination of the paint layers disclosed the composition of the paint, revealing that the original was a flesh-color tempera, the paint having been mixed with egg yolk and water. It was decided to remove the layer of brown oil overpaint. Before this could be done, however, all the paint—the original light tempera and the subsequent coat of dark brown oil pigment—had to be put back down securely. This was done with the use of a warm wax-resin adhesive. At this point, the dark brown could be removed, by means of gentle scraping with dental tools and scalpels. Next came the delicate problem of removing the fuel oil which had entered the tiny holes in the figure without destroying the original paint in the process. Before each new step, an up-to-date report was required from Dr. Plather's wife in the chemistry laboratory. It was learned that the best way to remove the oil was with the use of the mixture of sepiolite and a solvent, working on the principle of solvent and absorption.

There were daily problems in the restoration of this fragile work, but they were overcome, and *Saint Sebastian* was restored to its original beauty, as are so many objects when they leave the Palazzo Davanzati.

11

A Hospital for Books

The Certosa of Galluzzo stands high on a hill a few miles from Florence. It is a fourteenth-century Carthusian monastery, surrounded by rich olive groves and small farms. In summertime, busloads of tourists visit the monastery and the church, examine the art treasures by Della Robbia, Bronzino, and Luca Cranach, and buy the sweet liqueur made by the monks from herbs and grasses.

Though the setting may seem unlikely, it is here that the books from the Gabinetto Vieusseux are being restored. When the 250,000 volumes from the library had been removed from the Palazzo Strozzi, they were taken to dry out at a tobacco-drying plant; from there they were transported to the ancient monastery.

Everything about the "book hospital" at the Certosa seems improvised with intelligence and extreme ingenuity. The building itself, a prefabricated structure, was constructed alongside the monastery. Whatever was lacking in the way of facilities for the restoration of books, and this included almost everything, was built as needed by the carpenter from the library. Funds were scarce—the Vieusseux is a private library—so materials at hand were used, leftovers from former exhibitions, wood, and other materials that had been stored in the library.

Inside the hastily but intelligently built structure, men and women totally new to their jobs have worked another kind of miracle. Whatever their background or experience, they have responded where

*A book from the
Gabinetto Vieusseux
before restoration*

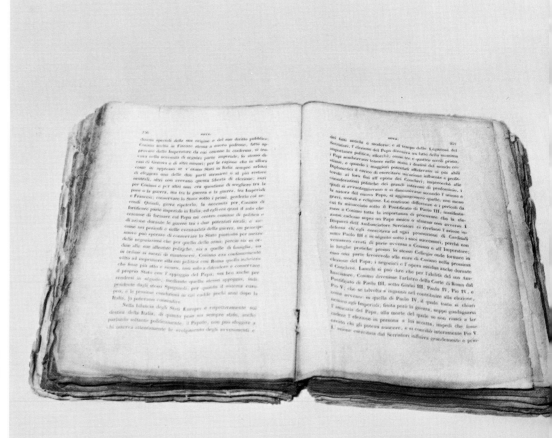

*The same book
after restoration*

needed. In charge of the technical restoration team is a warm, dedicated man, Mauro Fabbri, who before the flood worked on the magazines and bulletins put out by the library. In charge of the newly built chemical laboratory is Dr. Maurizio Copedé who was, before the flood, a professor of archeology. It is Dr. Copedé who experiments constantly with solutions to be used for cleaning the books in his small, hastily equipped laboratory. In the first weeks, this unassuming young professor discovered a new solvent for taking off mildew stains without dissolving the print of a book. And then Copedé, with his modest resources, made a most important discovery, a method of separating the pages of those books which were printed on coated, or glossy, paper. When these books were submerged in the water, the pages stuck together as if glued. Separation seemed impossible, but after a great deal of experimentation, Dr. Copedé came upon a new liquid solution so that now, after a book is soaked in the liquid for a few hours, the pages neatly separate. His is a remarkable contribution to book restoration, an example of a remedy devised out of necessity.

Dedication, pride, these are the most important elements felt at the Certosa. And a love and respect for books and what they mean. Books are everywhere, books looking like piles of clay or cement; they seem to be hopelessly lost, but they can be restored. They stand on the floor-to-ceiling metal shelves, they hang from the ceiling by strings. Piles of sodden books and valuable collections of newspapers and magazines are all about. There are loose pages, fragments, some as small as dollar bills, all of them able to respond to carefully worked-out, if improvised, methods of restoration.

The "hospital" is well organized after its initial trials. The first job has been to remove the covers of the books. Then the pages are strung up on metal racks to await washing, disinfecting—this to prevent the growth of mold—and individual restoration. The mud is cleaned off page by page, as a first step. Then the pages are carefully dried under a controlled temperature. Once dry, each book is individually catalogued by inventory numbers—author and title—and according to the special restoration involved for each volume. Then the individual restoration begins, according to a priority system established by Professor Bonsanti. This might involve further cleaning with stronger solutions; disinfection by injection or other means; and patching.

There is an air of excitement and enthusiasm in each room of this laboratory for the restoration of books. It is a sign of the belief of these people in what they are doing, in their role in the enormous job of preserving Florence's cultural heritage. No part is too small, for each is essential. Florence's libraries must again be a ready source of knowledge for scholars from all over the world.

In one room, at a small table, a young man is patiently patching pages together, using a warm iron to keep the fragments in place. Another room is for men working on newspapers. They are for the most part former workers from a textile plant. When the flood came, their factory was destroyed, and they found work at the Certosa. By the time their factory had been rebuilt, most chose to continue working on the precious books and newspapers. In another room, there are the volunteers doing the tedious but essential job of cleaning each book, page by page. There is a long table, in the midst of which is a tub containing the solution used in the cleaning. The volunteers, whose hands are covered with rubber gloves to prevent injury, dip a brush into the solution and carefully work the soft bristles against the pages. They must work cautiously and use gentle strokes; it is easy to do further damage to a book. The mud comes off relatively quickly, but the fuel oil can take up to an hour per page. Each day Dr. Copedé experiments further, hoping to add a new element to the solution that might make the job an easier one. As he continues his experiments, the volunteers go on with their job. It is not an exciting one, not an interesting one, but they know that what they are doing is important for all time. A large number of the volunteers have come from all over the world, people of all ages from France, Holland, Switzerland, England, and the United States. Some are spending their lifetime savings in order to remain in Florence to help; others have barely enough money to live on as they devotedly continue their tedious work. Their reasons for working at the Certosa might best

*Old manuscripts and modern printed matter hung up
to dry in lending room of Palazzo Strozzi*

be summed up in the words of Mrs. Cecily Spellman, a young American housewife who had come to Florence with her husband and four small children to enjoy and study the wonders of the city; and who found herself spending two long mornings a week cleaning books at the Certosa. She said: "I could work for ten years over the ruined pages and not repay Florence for the moments in San Lorenzo and the New Sacristy."

Professor Bonsanti and Dr. Fabbri hope and expect that more than ninety per cent of the books and newspapers in the Vieusseux will be saved. But it will take many years, perhaps as many as fifteen or twenty, a large amount of money, and an unflagging dedication to the work. It is a task well worth the effort.

The large majority of books and documents from the National Library that were damaged during the flood are being restored at the library itself. If personal dedication and ingenuity are the key features at the restoration center at the Certosa, then the operation at the National Library could best be characterized as a monument to modern technological development. Largely through the efforts of the Library's director, Dr. Emanuele Casamassima, in obtaining wide international support, the enormous job of restoring the Library's gigantic and priceless collection has proceeded with extraordinary efficiency and skill. Though improvisation has played a role in the work at the National Library—in the sense that the directors are never sure what is needed until it is needed, since there is no precedent for their work—the finest modern equipment available has been called into service.

What was in the days during and after the flood a slimy pool of paper, water, and mud has been converted into a huge modern laboratory, inhabited by hundreds of people, most of whom are new to their occupations. As at the Certosa, books in various shapes and forms are everywhere, together with loose pages, magazines, newspapers, and catalogue cards. Everything, however, is organized with the greatest skill and efficiency. At first, each book is photographed in its flood-damaged state. Then the binding and sewing of each volume are removed, and the sections—or signatures—separated. Next, each volume is collated and checked to see if individual pages are missing, torn or require special treatment. A unique system of symbols has been devised at the library by which all workers can recognize a book's specific problems: for example, an "X" means that "this book has blue marks, possibly of bacteriological origin," and three exclamation points means that "very careful attention is needed." In the latter case, a special note describing the treatment is appended.

Once the volume has thus been examined, the book is then washed (alcohol is often used to remove mud stains), deacidified, and each page is cleaned in a fungicide solution to protect the surface of the paper from mold. Mold comes in many varieties, and each responds to a different treatment, so special care must be taken. It is ironic that the mud which so ravaged Florence served to protect many books from more serious oil stains.

When a book has been cleaned and disinfected, excessive moisture is squeezed out in a press and the book, placed in open racks in signatures, is put into specially designed drying cabinets. Finally, after further disinfection in many cases, the signatures are reassembled and the book is ready for rebuilding.

A large part of the library has been mobilized for this task. The former main reading room of the library has become a workshop for repairing damaged pages. There is a special rare-book restoration laboratory, a periodical library and a department with one hundred hand looms for rebinding. Perhaps the enormity of the task can best be illustrated through figures.

Approximately 1,200,000 bibliographic units were damaged: 300,000 books, 20,000 titles of newspapers and magazines (each title refers to hundreds of copies), 60,000 volumes of bound magazines, 400,000 pieces of miscellany such as extracts and pamphlets, 50,000 volumes of French and German theses and eight million catalogue cards. Each item must be treated individually, with painstaking care and precision. Damage to the library building itself also was

*Student volunteers
interleaved the pages
of rare books*

*Book pages were individually
hung out to dry*

immense; fourteen and a half miles of shelving, 4,000 catalogue drawers, furniture, safes, office equipment; the heating, electrical, and air conditioning systems.

About 13,000 volumes have been sent out of Florence—to other Italian cities, to Vienna and to the British Museum, and help has come from all parts of the world. From America, the Xerox Corporation, represented by University Microfilms, has donated $50,000 worth of microfilm cameras and equipment as well as personnel to reproduce the 8 million catalogue cards after each has been dried out, sterilized and cleaned. Later the newspaper collection too will be microfilmed. Essential to the operation of restoration has been a team under the direction of a British expert, Peter Waters, a lecturer at the Royal College of Art in London. A part of the team is a young African, Joe Nkrumah, who was trained in Rome, Brussels, and London and who eventually plans to return to the National Museum in Accra. A truly international team, drawing on the finest resources from all over the world, will restore the National Library. But the job there, too, as at the Certosa and at the State Archives, where similar procedures are being followed, will be a long and costly one.

12

A Hospital for Paintings

The work going on at the Fortezza di Basso, an old military installation behind the Florence railroad station, is perhaps the most overwhelmingly impressive sight to be seen in Florence after the flood. In the six weeks following the flood, this collection of abandoned sheds, belonging to an old barracks, full of weeds and garbage, was converted into seven hangar-sized workshops, a temporary home for thousands of masterpieces, being treated by some sixty restoration specialists from ten countries. Working side by side are skilled scientists not only from all parts of Italy but from France, Russia, the Scandinavian countries, England, America, Switzerland, and Germany. Entering the Fortress is like setting foot in a combination clinic and architectural studio. There are spotless white walls, carefully controlled air conditioning and humidifying systems, and large drawing tables, covered with masterpieces of many centuries. These precious works of art, seemingly wounded, patched, and bandaged, are painstakingly treated by a many-lingual white-uniformed staff.

In terms of its contents and the people working there, this improvised but extraordinarily well-equipped laboratory is the most important in the world today. It is endowed with the most precious and rare equipment, sent from Moscow, Amsterdam, New York, and Berlin. It is the envy of foreign experts as a laboratory of the highest order, and the world's good wishes and hopes are focussed upon it.

Among the patients in this massive hospital are works by the greatest artists of all times—Giotto, Masaccio, Fra Angelico, Bot-

*Restoring a Velasquez
self-portrait*

Portrait of a Gentleman
by Velasquez

ticelli, and Fra Filippo Lippi—Florence's richest treasures, each under its own special treatment with its own doctor.

Immediately after the flood, none of the damaged works could be moved from their location, for a sudden change of temperature and humidity might have irreparably destroyed them. Thus, to prevent paint from falling off, they were stretched out horizontally in the museums and churches, where they awaited their destiny.

The major problems in those early days was to protect the paint and keep it from peeling off. This was of extreme urgency and had to be carried out at once; one single uniform treatment had to be decided upon, one that would be effective but would not prejudice any future operations that had to be carried out after further studies.

So it was that, while still in their museums and churches, the paintings were covered with a very fine sheet of Japanese rice paper, applied to the surface of the painting with an adhesive to prevent the peeling of the water-soaked layers of paint. Since a huge quantity of this rice paper was required, a world-wide appeal was made, and soon the paper began to arrive from every part of the world. But when, from time to time, supplies of the paper ran out, substitutes were used, including Kleenex, though that too was in short supply for most of Florence's drugstores had been flooded. This first operation was accomplished by more than twenty restorers from all over Italy, along with quickly trained student helpers.

Next, many of the paintings were sent to the Gallery of the Academy to receive the preliminary treatment of facing with a protective covering and then disinfection. Other paintings on canvas as well as the more fragile paintings on wood were transferred to what could be considered an emergency ward in the Limonaia, a huge greenhouse in the Boboli Gardens, behind the Pitti Palace. This immense building, 120 yards long and ten yards high, is normally used to house and cultivate, under controlled conditions, the collection of lemon trees of the Pitti Palace. In little over a week it was converted to an emergency hospital for paintings, equipped with a stockroom for materials and wooden stands for the paintings. The walls and windows were specially insulated, and a heating and humidifying system created in which the paintings could remain in a temperature of 50 degrees Fahrenheit and at a humidity of either 85% or 95%, to prevent further damage, to stop the wood from drying out too quickly and to check the loosening of the priming, or first coat, and with it the painted surfaces. Here the paintings lay, spotted with rice paper, treated with antibiotics to prevent mold, awaiting the diagnosis which would lead to further specialized individual treatment.

By July the great laboratory at the Fortezza di Basso was operating and the first paintings were delivered there. Most were merely to have their paint stabilized, that is to have the loose paint reattached, or to be firmly attached to their supports with glue or wax. The actual restoration—that is, the cleaning and repainting of missing areas—is to be done at a later time, after the threat of the paint coming loose from its base has been completely eliminated. By being stabilized and covered with paper, the paintings can await definitive restoration without fear of further damage.

By far the most difficult problem is presented by the paintings mounted on wood. These consist of several levels, of different materials: the wood support, a canvas stretched and often glued to it, a first, or priming, layer of plaster and glue and finally the painting itself. The flood waters caused the wood to swell, stretching the canvas and priming, which in turn tends to dissolve and loosen the paint. In other cases, the paint itself, because of the uneven traction of the wood base, widens its cracks, dilates, loosens, and peels off.

Day after day, the skilled specialists from all over the world, with the use of the finest scientific equipment available, watched over these patients, the masterpieces which were undergoing very slow but inexorable chemical and physical changes beneath the surface. Their first job was to protect against, slow down, and reverse these changes.

As the wood swells—one ten-foot-long painting increased more than five inches in length—the plaster swells too, creating large bubbles of color. Since these distortions, warping, weakening, or disintegration on the canvas, did not die out after drying, it was necessary in several cases actually to remove the painting from its old support and transfer it to a new one, of canvas or of wood.

This is an extremely delicate operation, and the risks involved are great. The first step is to protect the painted surface with a double layer of rice paper; then a canvas soaked in plaster and glue is stretched over it as reinforcement. Next, the painting is turned over on its face so that the useless, diseased wood support may be removed. A vibration-free electric plane is then used to cut away most of the wood. As the back of the painting itself is approached, the restorers begin to use gouges and lancets, working delicately under microscopes. When the priming is reached, the same technique used by the original artist, determined by intricate laboratory tests, is repeated to reinforce it, after which the painting is applied to a new wood support, one that is wormproof, stable, and absorbent.

The work of stabilizing all the paintings will take a few years; final restoration and cleaning will continue for many more years. And even then, when restoration is completed, a careful study will have to be made of the environment, whether it be a museum or a church, to which the painting will be returned, so that each work may be accustomed to the temperature of its home before it is returned there.

On the top floor of the Fortezza, other "patients" are being stored, attached to metallic screens running parallel down a huge corridor. These are the magnificent frescoes, the wall paintings, of Florence, damaged in the flood in a way no one had predicted. In fact, it wasn't until two months after the flood that restoration experts realized that frescoes which had not even felt the full impact of the flood waters were being attacked and threatened by the salts, sodium and potassium nitrate, with which the flood waters were saturated. The water which had been absorbed in the walls of the churches was climbing up these painted walls by capillary action and, in its slow ascension, was leaving behind the salts which crystallized on the surface of the walls, forming a miniscule volcano which tended to explode. For this reason, a huge number of works were unexpectedly threatened.

Madonna With Child
and Saints,
*a triptych by Straus,
recovered in the Church
of Santa Maria Novella,
being restored by technicians*

*Removing the mud from
a painting*

*Restorers salvaging a painting
in the Uffizi Gallery*

The deadly salts were eating away the paint of the frescoes.

This was a completely new problem for the restorers, one which had to be faced quickly and with the assistance of competent scientists. Fortunately, the spread of this disease could be stopped; the solution was found by professors of physical and organic chemistry at the University of Florence who suggested the use of tributilphosphate which held the salts back and stopped their crystallization.

But the damaged frescoes had to be detached from their walls, in most cases, in order to be restored, and this too presented great and delicate problems.

Two thousand years ago, when the ancient Romans imported parts of frescoes from Greece, they had to take most of the walls on which they were painted along with them. Today, through a technique known as "strapo," the paint surface alone can be pulled away, and none of the pigment is lost. This is accomplished by coating the fresco with a thick solution of a special glue and then covering it with a gauzelike canvas. When the glue has dried, the canvas is carefully rolled up, successfully removing the fresco without damage. In this way, a fourteenth-century work, Nardo di Cione's fresco of the *Inferno*, measuring 1,215 square feet, was detached from the walls of the Strozzi Chapel of the church of Santa Maria Novella, thereby becoming the largest fresco ever to be detached in one piece. And Taddeo Gaddi's masterpiece, *The Tree of the Cross*, measuring 1,100 square feet, was detached, rolled up like a carpet and taken from its home at Santa Croce. All in all, almost 20,000 square feet of frescoes were removed from their walls. Then the great fight against the humidity, mildew, and the new threat of the salts began in the laboratories, set up under the direction of fifty specialists, at the Refectory of S. Salvi and at the Limonaia. First the remains of the backing of the walls, up to the very painting itself, had to be removed; next, the works had to be remounted on stable supports; and finally came the removal of the adhesives and protective canvases preparatory to the actual restoration of the frescoes.

In removing the magnificent frescoes from the walls of the

*Restorers working
at the Limonaia*

churches of Florence, however, one positive element came to light. Beneath two thirds of the detached frescoes were found the original sketches for these frescoes. These are called sinopias, since they were drawn with a reddish-brown earth color from Sinope on the Black Sea. The discovery of more than three hundred of them is of major importance; they are certainly the works of the masters themselves, while the actual frescoes based on these preliminary drawings were frequently executed by assistants in the artist's workshop.

The sinopias, too, were moved to the restoration center at the Fortezza da Bazzo, and plans are underway to exhibit these newly discovered masterpieces in the Pitti Palace. In this way, the terrible flood has increased the artistic patrimony of Florence.

13

The Chapel of San Luca

Piazza Santissima Annunziata is one of the liveliest in Florence, and on March 25th, Annunciation Day, it is the scene of a gay Florentine fair, where brightly colored objects and foods of every variety, from chestnuts to cotton candy, are sold. Facing the square is one of the Florentines' favorite churches, the church of Santissima Annunziata, a fifteenth-century building dedicated to the miraculous Annunciation.

March 25th celebrates the day on which the angel Gabriel announced to the Virgin Mary that she would be the mother of the Messiah.

On March 25th, 1968, ·visitors swarmed the square as usual. Many passed the elderly dark-clothed women selling candles and entered the church to worship. Even on this holiday workmen were busily going about their jobs and repairing damage to the church which had been filled with five to six feet of water at the height of the flood. Some people entered a door to the left of the main entrance, passed through the courtyard and went into the small Chapel of San Luca (Saint Luke). The chapel still showed many signs of the flood. Detached from the walls were two important frescoes, Bronzino's *Deposition* and Pontormo's *Madonna with Four Saints*; these had been removed when, overnight, salts from the flooded area had begun to crawl up the walls, by capillary action, and threaten these two sixteenth-century masterpieces, which were now being restored in a restoration studio. Religious objects such as ornate candlesticks had been removed from the altarpiece. The floor was scarred and dirty. And in a corner, high on a ladder, stood a slender young girl, patiently and lovingly cleaning one of the sculptures.

With her long hair tied back, and her almost angelic features, the girl did not look out of place in the small Renaissance chapel. The work this 23-year-old American girl was doing was something she would remember with pride the rest of her life.

Anne Boardman had first come to Florence in 1962, when she was eighteen, after graduation from a girl's school in Connecticut. She spent a year there, first studying Italian, then studying art, history, and sculpture at the Florentine Academy of Fine Arts. After that year, she returned to her native Rhode Island and entered the Rhode Island School of Design. Her interest in sculpture grew and so did her nostalgia for Florence, the city which had opened her eyes to the wonders of art. When the flood came, she was in the midst of her last year in school. The Committee to Rescue Italian Art was being organized largely by professors from the Providence area, among them Bates Lowry and Frederick Leicht, and Anne did all she could to help, working long after-school hours. More and more, she was worried by the news from her beloved Florence; helping out in an office in Providence, Rhode Island, just wasn't enough. Her plans to go to graduate school at the University of Wisconsin seemed suddenly insignificant, and she pleaded with the directors of the American Committee to send her to Florence. The answer was a disappointing no.

Months passed, and Anne continued to hope that she might somehow get to Florence to help restore her adopted city. Finally, in the spring of 1967, CRIA received funds from which to allocate grants to send student workers to Florence. Because she knew Italian, because she knew Florence, and because of her interest in sculpture and her knowledge of its material—and most probably because of her enormous enthusiasm—Anne Boardman was chosen among the many hundreds of applicants to go to Florence as a CRIA fellow. On June 4th, she received her Bachelor of Fine Arts; on June 5th she was on the plane to Florence.

Once there, she was sent to the Restoration Center for Sculpture and Minor Arts at the Palazzo Davanzati and interviewed by the Directress, who took note of the young American's special interests and qualifications. At first, she was put to work on the cleaning of marble sculpture from the Bargello, the National Museum. Then, one day, Kenneth Hempel, chief restorer at the Victoria and Albert Museum in London, came to Davanzati on one of his frequent visits. He felt the time had come to begin work on the restoration of the sculptures in the Chapel of San Luca. Funds had been granted for this job by CRIA at the instigation of Professor Curtis Shell, head of the Department of Art History at Wellesley College in Massachusetts, who had been in Florence at the time of the flood. Hempel asked who would be best qualified to undertake a job that would require sculpture remodeling; the Directress of the restoration center suggested Anne Boardman.

With her usual enthusiasm, Anne went about finding out all she could about the history of this small chapel, one often ignored by visitors to Florence. She learned that the chapel had been built in 1496; and that it was later chosen by the Academy of Design as its place of worship (Saint Luke was the patron saint of painters).

During the years from 1560 to 1575, the Chapel had been remodeled under the auspices of the Academy. As a part of the remodeling of the Chapel, the Academy had had a lottery, as a result of which it had given various artists commissions for the original twelve statues. The effective head of the Academy at its start in 1562 was Michelangelo, and one of the Academy's first duties was to stage, in 1564, the magnificent funeral of Michelangelo. Because of its history and association, the chapel was known as the Painters' Chapel; beneath it lie the tombs of Pontormo and Benvenuto Cellini, among many other famed architects, sculptors, and painters.

Anne's primary job in the Chapel of San Luca was to restore the ten sculptures which lined three of the walls (of the twelve original statues, two are missing), that is, to bring them back to their original condition. The statues represent Saint Luke, Melchisedek (King of Salem), Cosimo I, Saint John the Evangelist, Saint Paul, Moses, Abra-

*The Chapel of San Luca,
before the flood*

*Anne Boardman restoring
an unbaked-clay statue
in the Chapel of San Luca*

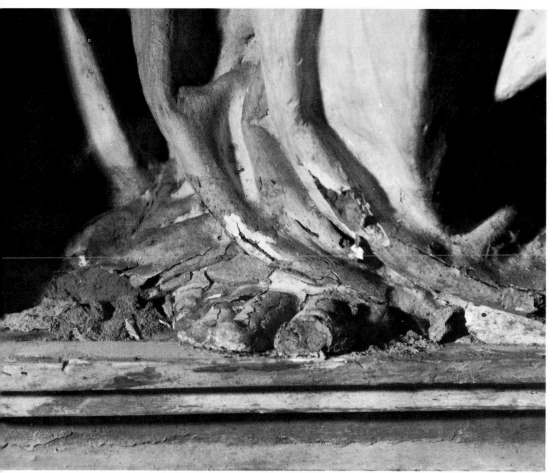

*The condition of the foot
of one of the statues
after the flood*

*After restoration,
a statue looked like this*

ham, David, Solomon, and Saint Peter. The first seven were executed in unbaked clay (also known as terra non cotta) which was often used by Florentine sculptors in the sixteenth century. Using this unbaked clay, the sculptor would model a statue that would later be carved from marble in his workshop. These works in the Chapel of San Luca were never executed in marble and thus remained in their "model" state; for this reason, they could be considered actually more "original" than finished works in marble.

The clay was modeled directly on a prepared wooden armature, or supporting framework, and in areas where additional support was necessary, straw and burlap were mixed into the clay. They would serve to bind the clay together and keep it in place. When the clay was finally dried, a gesso preparation (usually a gypsum ground) was applied to the surface, which was then painted.

When the flood water rushed into the Chapel of San Luca, these seven unbaked clay statues, because of the nature of their material, were most seriously damaged; fortunately they were placed well above the ground so that only the feet were actually hit by the waters. But when the waters hit, the dried clay expanded and caused the surface preparation to crack and flake off. When completely soaked in the water, the clay crumbled and through the force of the waters, suspended areas separated and fell off the statues.

Under the supervision of Kenneth Hempel, Anne Boardman began work on the statues. First, the flood-damaged areas were scraped clean and then consolidated by means of an Epoxy resin, a synthetic plastic in a liquid state, which was combined with a hardener, called a catalyst. This was painted on the damaged surface with small brushes and, in some cases, injected into weak areas with a syringe. With the aid of heating lamps to quicken the process, the resin and catalyst would solidify the weakened areas within an hour. Then came the remodeling, where the surface was either lost or uneven, with the use of a very strong, non-shrinkable, water-resistant plaster from England. Next step was to reapply the gesso preparation, and finally the statue was retouched, or brought back to its original color.

Anne Boardman working on small sculpture from the Chapel of San Luca

But there were many problems, common to all sculptural restoration. Though only the feet of these statues had been directly damaged by the flood, it was decided to clean each statue completely. It was determined after microscopic tests, that the surface, under the dirt, was of a yellow tempera (the color mixed with egg yoke and water) that had been painted in a previous restoration in 1823. This yellow paint was not only weak: it was not in keeping with the original spirit of the chapel, so a decision was made to remove it and return the statues to their original sixteenth-century colors. Analysis showed that the original paint underneath the 1823 restoration was strong, so the careful, long job of removing the top layer of yellow tempera by means of gentle scraping with surgical blades was begun.

Other problems arose; removal of the top layer revealed a poor earlier restoration of the right elbow of Saint John the Evangelist. So, drawing upon her training in sculpture, it became Anne's responsibility to remould this elbow according to the original lines of the sculpture. In August 1967, the first sculpture—that of Saint Luke—was completed. At the end of the month, Anne Boardman was to return to Rhode Island, but she was asked to stay on another year to complete her work on the Chapel of San Luca. When the Chapel of San Luca is finally restored to its former beauty, much credit must be given to this young girl from Rhode Island, whose skill and patience typify the spirit which will bring about a new renaissance in Florence.

Epilogue

On the night of November 3rd, 1967, exactly one year after the flood waters began their descent on Florence, a most unusual parade was held. It began with a gathering of young people from all over the world, those courageous students who had come to the rescue of Florence in its days of need.

The students met at the Church of San Miniato al Monte, an ancient church on a hill above the city. In the church's courtyard, torches were handed out and lighted, and the group began to march down into the town. As they proudly paraded towards the river, they sang songs of every nation. They passed through the district of San Niccolò, where crowds gathered along the streets, windows were opened, and applause rang out.

The torchlight parade continued, across the river and into Piazza Santa Croce, where a large crowd of that section's inhabitants stood ready to cheer and applaud these young people who had done so much to save their homes and, in some cases, their lives. There followed a moving ceremony, after which the students returned to the river. Once there, to the accompaniment of shouts of protest and defiance, they hurled their lighted torches into the Arno. This was their way to show anger and contempt for a river that had nearly destroyed the city of Florence.

This would be a good note on which to end this story of the Florence flood and its aftermath; it would provide a happy, positive ending to a tragic episode in history. Unfortunately, there can be no such ending, for a great deal remains to be done.

For one thing, these very students are full of resentment. The same issue of the Florence newspaper which reported the torchlight parade carried an item which described the turning away of long-haired students who had come to the city to participate in a protest demonstration at the university. No noisy demonstrations, the paper reported, would be tolerated. It is for this reason that so many of Florence's students are bitter. The world knows that in the days following the flood they spontaneously turned out in full force and made a major contribution towards the salvation of a cultural heritage. They had worked unselfishly day and night, and wherever they went—no matter what the length of their hair or of their beards—they were welcomed as saviors. They were called "the angels of the mud," or "the blue angels" (because so many wore blue jeans), and their elders marvelled at their courage and energy. Yet, one year later, these same "heroes" were being turned away from the very city that they helped to save. They wonder, too, why the police and city officials, who they felt were slow to come to the rescue of the flooded city, are so quick to come when students gather to protest against what they feel to be injustices, either at their schools or in their world.

At the height of a student demonstration at the University of Florence, a university official said he hoped the excesses of a minority of students would not imperil those cultural goods which had been saved the year before by the "angels of the mud." "We laughed when he said that," said Tommaso Detti, "but it was serious. The students who helped save the libraries last year are the same ones—with some exceptions—who today are demonstrating to change the university, and to some extent society itself. They are the ones who are interested, concerned. This university official was trying to separate two things that go together. Students are good when they save a library and bad when they demonstrate. . . ."

It was indeed the concerned people who helped Florence during its dark days. This is true not only among students but among those of their parents' generation, for the same people who years before had led the struggle against Mussolini and Fascism were the leaders of the battle against the flood.

Florence depends on its young people for its future; a long and difficult job remains to be done, and the city cannot expect its young citizens to help if they are not shown the respect they so richly earned at the time of the crisis. These young people will, in turn, learn to respect their city and its officials as soon as efficient and progressive methods are adopted to prevent future floods and deal with the many social and economic problems that have been brought to light by the flood and its aftermath.

"Il Bisonte," Maria Luigia Guaita's workshop, is fully active again.

Lithographs recovered from the mud and slime were washed, dried and ironed out by her nephew Enrico and his friends—another example of the work done, this time on a personal level, by the young people of Florence. These restored lithographs were then sold at special exhibitions in Rome, Bologna, and at the Fleisher-Anhalt Gallery in Los Angeles, California. Within a month after the flood, the presses and whatever other equipment remained intact were moved to a temporary workshop in another part of Florence. But a return to San Niccolò was essential, to give new courage to those people there who had lost it, and Maria Luigia Guaita proudly reopened her gallery and workshop on via San Niccolò one year after the flood.

Sad to report, however, is the fact that a large number of the artisans, small shopkeepers, and craftsmen were wiped out and will never recover from the cruel damages inflicted by the flood. It is estimated that some six thousand of them lost their tools, materials, and workshops. Many of them are too old to begin again; those self-employed workers who were able to have left the district of San Niccolò and others like it, and have taken factory jobs. If this were to mean the end of the fine craftsmanship of Florence, it would be a serious loss for the city as well as for the world, which has derived so much pleasure from

*Maria Luigia Guaita
in the reception room
of Il Bisonte, April, 1968*

*Maria Luigia Guiata
with her assistants.
The workshop is reborn*

the products of the skill and imagination of the Florentine artisan.

The future of Florence's books and art treasures, too, is not yet secure. If miracles have been accomplished since the flood, it is nonetheless true that more miracles must be performed in the future. It has been estimated that a single restorer would have to work two hundred and ten consecutive years to restore completely the paintings on wood and on canvas that were disfigured by the oily waters. There is, of course, more than a single restorer working in Florence today, so this merely represents a statistical curiosity. However, it does show the need for the continued support of governments and private organizations and individuals in the fight to save Florence. The vast amount of money and technical assistance—in the form of equipment and personnel—that was offered to Florence in those harrowing days after the flood bears witness to the world's concern and the love it feels towards Florence. But now when the first dramatic and emotional impact has disappeared, the need is no less great and contributions of every sort must be continued. The job ahead is a challenging one, and aid to Florence must not slacken.

One final question remains: Can it happen again? Florentines are, with good reason, frightened of the water, of their own river. "Every noise frightens me," said a five-year-old boy. "I always say, it will pass. And the days go on, but I am no longer the same." Another child has written of the Arno: "It frightens people. . . . It breaks parapets, it makes houses collapse. It brings destruction."

The answer to the question is yes, and the fear felt not only by young children is justified. The same river which nearly caused the destruction of mankind's great treasure could rise again and cause even greater destruction. The threat from the Arno's waters has been with Florence since the times of the Romans. Even Leonardo da Vinci was concerned with the problem; included in one of his recently discovered notebooks is a drawing of a plan to control the river. Yet it seems that Florentines have been consoled by the fact that these floods occur at long intervals and very rarely reach disaster proportions.

The flood of 1966 was the most serious in the history of Florence,

Eighteen months after
the flood, recovery work
continues at San Niccoló

March, 1968.
The work of recovery continues
inside Santa Croce

Almost two years after
the flood, the peaceful
Arno plays host to sportsmen
while the work of
reconstruction continues

and there is no certainty that the waters will not rise again in the near future. For this reason, it is hard to understand why so little has been done, since 1966, to prevent future floods, why modern technological skills have not been put to full use. The problems are admittedly great, and the complete success of any method of flood prevention cannot be guaranteed because of Florence's precarious geographical position at the bottom of a valley. However, a few basic steps can be taken. New forests to check erosion are the basis of any struggle against floods, yet new forests have not been planted. No new dikes have been completed, new dams have not been built, and no provision has been made to free the excessive water flowing into the shallow Arno basin during the rainy season. The river banks and foundations have not been sufficiently reinforced. Funds seem to be lacking for these measures, yet they are available for less vital ones.

The finest creative talent and modern technological methods have been used unsparingly in the restoration of Florence. Should they not also be employed to make certain that the destruction of this priceless artistic heritage and the immeasurable human loss will not happen again?

Though such serious problems remain to be faced, it is nevertheless heartening that the world, and especially its young generation, concerned as it is with the possibilities of the future, recognized its debt to the past, to its heritage, and gave so generously to save the treasures of Florence.

woman on Lungaro Corsini. The Ponte Vecchio is in the background

PHOTOGRAPH CREDITS

1. Palazzo Pandolfini
2. San Marco
3. Mercato Centrale
4. Palazzo Medici-Riccardi
5. Medici Chapel
6. Santa Maria Maggiore
7. San Gaetano
8. Santa Maria Novella
9. San Pancrazio
10. Palazzo Strozzi
11. Palazzo Rucellai
12. Ognissanti
13. San Paolino
14. Palazzo Corsini
15. Santa Trinita
16. Palazzo Guicciardini
17. Caserma Generale Sani
18. San Frediano in Cestello
19. Santa Maria del Carmine
20. Palazzo Amerighi
21. Santo Spirito
22. Palazzo Guadagni
23. Palazzo dei Frescobaldi
24. Santi Apostoli
25. Palazzo Davanzati
26. Mercato Nuovo
27. Orsanmichele
28. Baptistry
29. Giotto's Campanile
30. Santa Maria del Fiore (Duomo)
31. Ospedale di Santa Maria Nuova (Hospital)
32. Santa Maria degli Angioli
33. Museo Archeologico
34. Santissima Annunziata
35. Galleria dell'Accademia di Belle Arti
36. Teatro della Pergola